Mindfulness Made Simple

Mindfulness Made Simple

An Introduction to Finding Calm Through Mindfulness & Meditation

FOREWORD BY ELISHA GOLDSTEIN, PH.D.

CALISTOGA
PRESS

Get Started Right Away

YOUR FIRST MEDITATION

Preparation

Create a supportive and comfortable environment for your first meditation. SEE PAGE 37

Posture

Settle into a comfortable position. SEE PAGE 51

Meditation

Allow your body to relax and bring your attention to the breath. SEE PAGE 52

Reflection

Spend a few moments letting yourself reconnect to the world around you. SEE PAGE 54

YOUR MINDFULNESS PRACTICE

Intention

Set an intention to make mindfulness a part of your daily life. SEE PAGE 5

Pause

Take a deep breath and notice how you feel at this exact moment. SEE PAGE 7

Practice

Pick a simple activity and do it mindfully. SEE PAGE 74

CONTENTS

FOREWORD

THERE'S NO QUESTION ABOUT IT. Mindfulness is fast becoming one of the most-researched and most-talked-about phenomena today. Learning how to intentionally engage with the now is no longer considered a dubious pathway to an abstract enlightenment. Instead, it is backed by rigorous science as a practical way to open your mind to choices and possibilities that you may have never thought existed.

In the pages that follow, you'll begin a journey to discover that you can become naturally flexible in your decision making, regulate your body in moments of distress, calm your anxious mind when it's snowballing with thoughts, have greater focus at home and work, feel empathy and compassion toward yourself and others, communicate more effectively, and be more aware of what is most important to you.

Millions of people, including professionals in mental health, medicine, education, business, sports, and even politics have begun integrating mindfulness into our culture. Google, one of the most successful companies in the world, offers a program to help its employees hone their ability to be more present. Many healthcare companies are instituting courses in engaging with the now for their employees and corporate clients. A growing number of elementary, middle, and high schools are teaching their children mindfulness practices. Mindfulness is currently being used to help our military and its veterans. Amid the chaos of Capitol Hill, Congressman Tim Ryan of Ohio has created some reprieve with Quiet Time Caucus, where members go to get quiet. In sports,

Phil Jackson, arguably the most successful NBA coach of all time, always encouraged his players to practice mindful basketball, and the Seattle Seahawks, recent NFL champions, had a steady mindfulness practice. You can find mindfulness classes in thousands of recovery programs, mental health centers, and hospitals around the globe. The list goes on and on.

Why is this mindful revolution happening?

Many people point to a natural need to balance the overwhelming pressures we are experiencing in this day and age. Other people point to the explosion of neuroscience over the past decade, showing that we can use our minds to change our brains. This is incredibly empowering. The practical benefits that millions of people have experienced with mindfulness are hitting a tipping point.

In all the years that I've been practicing mindfulness, it has become very clear to me that mindfulness is the essential thread that keeps me grounded, clear, and able to focus on what really matters in my life. It's as if, over time, I have trained my brain to know when I'm imbalanced and to draw upon natural ways to rebalance. This has been instrumental in helping with my stress, my relationships, and my life. Don't get me wrong—this doesn't mean I don't get stressed, or angry, or imbalanced. It just means I recognize it sooner and am able to recalibrate with greater perspective.

Along the way I've learned four tips that have become integral to the way I practice, and I hope they will support you as you get started.

It's simple, but not easy. I've learned that while the teaching of mindfulness can be simple, it's not always so easy to practice. As we attempt to weave it in, our mind pops up to say that we're too busy, skeptical, or just unmotivated. Don't be alarmed: these are the mind's avoidance strategies. Just note them and come back to the practice.

Your practice is not a performance. Each practice doesn't need to be evaluated as a "good" meditation or a "bad" meditation. This performance-based mindset misses the point entirely. If there is any goal at all to these practices it's simply to learn. Bringing a learning mindset is the fastest route to growth and mastery.

You'll be imperfect at this—like the rest of us—and that's okay. If time goes by and you forget to practice, just "forgive and invite." Forgive yourself for the time gone by, investigate what took you off course, learn from it, and then in that space of awareness, invite yourself to begin again.

Acknowledging your effort matters. Remember, you are an active participant in your health and well-being. Every time you choose to engage in mindfulness it is with the intention of loving yourself. Perhaps the most important thing you can do is acknowledge yourself for making the effort to take time out of the daily hustle for your own learning, health, and well-being.

Now it's time to take a breath and get started. I wish you all the best as you begin this playful adventure into your life.

Elisha Goldstein, PhD
SANTA MONICA, CALIFORNIA

"Discovering how to be continuously present with each and every one of your experiences will enhance, and may even change, your life."

INTRODUCTION

Often called "paying attention on purpose," the practice of mindfulness guides us to focus on the present moment with nonjudgmental awareness. *Mindfulness Made Simple* offers an accessible way to bring this modern practice with ancient roots into your daily life. The basic elements of mindfulness practice—the body, the breath, and the mind—work together to help us shift from living life on "autopilot" to living in the moment. Practicing mindfulness can help resolve many concerns that distress us, including pain, anxiety, stress, insomnia, and other challenges of modern life.

Based on the latest wisdom in the field of mindfulness practice, this essential handbook introduces the theory and historical underpinnings of mindfulness and offers inspiring yet practical guidance for:

- Beginning your own mindfulness practice
- Applying mindfulness to particular concerns
- Incorporating mindfulness into your everyday life
- Deepening your mindfulness practice
- Investigating resources for further information

Mindfulness Made Simple is structured so that you can use it in the way that works best for you. Follow the book from beginning to end, learning some background about mindfulness and advancing step by step in the practice of mindfulness meditation, or simply start with basic meditations and then proceed to more advanced practices. You may decide to select meditations that are tailored to address particular issues that concern you. Or you can focus on the ways in which mindfulness can be brought into your everyday life. You decide what works for you.

Throughout the book, you will find exercises, tips, and journal prompts to help guide and facilitate your mindfulness practice:

- **Exercises** are specific, step-by-step procedures for practicing mindfulness. Much like physical exercise, the more you practice, the more these habits will feel natural and become part of your life.

- **Tips** will help you understand what to expect as you proceed in your mindfulness practice. Much like a human guide, they will help resolve some concerns you might have, address obstacles you are experiencing, and suggest ways to make your practice more useful.

- **Journal prompts** provide thoughts or ideas to consider as you progress in your mindfulness practice. If you decide to keep a journal of your mindfulness journey, prompts can help focus your thoughts as you begin to write about your feelings and accomplishments.

You will also find a comprehensive list of resources—from in-person instruction to audio meditations and more—to help you deepen your mindfulness practice. These are listed in the back of the book; feel free to consult them at any point in your practice.

To reference a well-known piece of ancient wisdom, you can begin your journey with a single step: Commit to learning about the practice of mindfulness. Discovering how to be continuously present with each and every one of your experiences will enhance, and may even change, your life. Within this book—and, more important, within yourself—you'll find everything you need to get started.

PART ONE
Understanding Mindfulness

_____

We have only this moment, sparkling like a star in our hand, and melting like a snowflake.

—Sir Francis Bacon, Sr.

CHAPTER ONE

What Is Mindfulness and How Does It Work?

Mindfulness as a practice refers to the conscious intention to be present in every moment of your life. Without requiring any particular beliefs or traditions, mindfulness is simply a way to notice thoughts, physical sensations, sights, sounds, smells, and reactions. As human beings, we are wired to continuously scan our thoughts and our environment for worries or threats. Through the use of mindfulness, we can shift from this routine to a consciousness in which we are *observing* our perceptions rather than merely *reacting* to them. This altered way of thinking and interacting with our environment may seem simple, yet it's a radical shift that can have powerful consequences.

Mindfulness helps us become more fully aware of our internal and external experiences. This can have a significant impact on our ability to:

- Relax physically
- Increase our self-awareness
- Maintain our emotional balance
- Regulate our behavior
- Minimize our self-criticism
- Decrease our stress
- Improve our relationships

Mindfulness is a learnable skill. Shifting attention from the past or the future to the present moment is usually cultivated through the practice of *mindfulness meditation*. Practicing mindfulness can help us recognize the typical and habitual patterns our thoughts follow, and to respond in new and less reactive ways. It encourages us to be sensitive to each moment, and to be open and receptive to our actual experience rather than our interpretation of that experience.

The Concepts

Although the practice of mindfulness meditation is closely associated with the state of mindfulness, mindfulness and meditation are not the same thing. We can think of mindfulness as a *way to be* and mindfulness meditation as a *way to do*.

Mindfulness

It is helpful to keep in mind two essential elements of mindfulness: attention and acceptance.

Attention

The choice to live mindfully means paying attention to your experiences as each one unfolds. This involves being aware of your thoughts, emotions, and sensations when they are happening. It means living consciously and deliberately, approaching each moment as though it might be the final moment. It also means that everything you do—speaking, eating, playing, walking, working, connecting with others—is done mindfully, from the perspective that each and every aspect of your life requires your attention in that moment.

EXERCISE **Simply Noticing**

For a brief time, look away from this book. You can keep your eyes open, looking down, or gently closed. Now just observe your present experience. Pay attention to how your body feels. Is it tense or relaxed, comfortable or in pain? Allow yourself to notice whatever physical sensations you are experiencing right now. Don't try to change or control what is happening. Instead, let it unfold. As you do this just for an instant, you are beginning to experience mindfulness.

TIP *When doing an exercise, read it several times and then put the instructions aside before you begin. If you forget the instructions, just notice that, too. Mindfulness is not about perfection. It is about being aware of the experience, including its imperfections.*

Acceptance

From a mindfulness standpoint, practicing acceptance means being able to perceive one's own experience clearly without judging it. For example, you might notice that you have a feeling of tightness in the calf of your leg. You could judge the experience negatively, thinking, *Oh no, something awful is happening to my body; I'd better go to the doctor,* or positively, with *Oh yeah, I can tell I had a serious workout yesterday.* But with mindful acceptance, you simply think, *Oh, there is tightness in my calf.*

This practice of acceptance is based on an absence of judgment, and is neither critical nor approving. It is simply perceiving what is and learning to let it be. When we allow ourselves to see experiences with clarity that is unclouded by judgments, we're better able to make decisions based on what actually *is*, rather than reacting to what we fear or fantasize might be.

With mindfulness, we can accurately recognize our mental landscape and increase our problem-solving ability. We might then think, *Perhaps I'll check out the source of that feeling in my leg and see if I need to do anything further,* or *Perhaps I'll wait to see if the tightness is gone tomorrow.* Whatever we decide, by first observing and accepting the reality of our experiences, we can bring balance and equanimity to our choices.

Mindfulness Meditation

Mindfulness meditation offers a way to learn and practice mindfulness. In other words, it is a tool that trains the mind to focus attention. Although there are many different forms of meditation—such as meditating on a word or phrase, or on a particular image or visualization—mindfulness meditation is a particular practice in which the goal is to become more aware, more connected to your body, breath, and mind in the present moment. Although mindfulness meditation may begin with a point of focus or concentration, as is common in many other meditative techniques, mindfulness meditation actually centers on the nonjudgmental observation of whatever then arises. Beginning with concentrated meditation, however, can help you actively observe conscious experiences and enhance your insight into these observations.

In the practice of mindfulness meditation, you note your thoughts and feelings *as a witness*, without guiding, ignoring, suppressing, evaluating, analyzing, or censoring these thoughts and feelings. You simply experience them as they happen. Mindfulness is not thoughtlessness, but it strives to create a different relationship with our thoughts. If you encounter a stressful thought, feeling, or sensation in the present moment, in mindfulness meditation you do not try to escape the unpleasantness, no matter how strong the impulse is to do so. You just attempt to perceive the thought, feeling, or sensation clearly and accept it as it is. This accepting awareness results, paradoxically, in greater clarity about what you actually think and feel. As you allow your thoughts to ebb and flow, you can become more fully aware of their content and how you react to it. You can develop insight into your feelings, the way you see the world, and what frightens you or what moves you. You can learn to distinguish between who you may have been prone to *think* you are and who you *actually* are. You can feel refreshed, inspired, and empowered as you enhance your receptivity to your reality.

A Brief History of Mindfulness

With a long history in many cultures, mindfulness is an idea that transcends both spiritual and secular thought. In Buddhist traditions, the notion of mindfulness has long been considered key to realizing the true nature of reality and the end of suffering. The word *mindfulness* is a common translation of the term *sati* from the Indo-Aryan language of Pali and is a part of many discussions by the historical Buddha. Modern Buddhist teacher Thích Nhất Hạnh says that right mindfulness is at the core of Buddhist practice. Other Eastern thought systems, including Hinduism and Taoism, have considered mindfulness to be a central element of spiritual practice. In the West, the ancient Greek Stoics addressed mindfulness as a critical philosophical tenet.

Generally, though, Western thought has tended to focus on the importance of mindfulness in more recent history. In the nineteenth century, American Transcendentalists, Henry David Thoreau among them, believed that life principles could be learned from conscious observation and emphasized the value of awareness and living life more deliberately. Early twentieth-century psychologist William James proposed that our subjective experience is actually composed only of what we notice. In the 1940s, Gestalt psychologists incorporated mindfulness into their therapeutic practice. Later twentieth-century humanistic psychologists replaced psychoanalytic approaches to problem solving with theories that considered the lived experience as a valuable way of knowing.

In the late 1970s, American molecular biologist Jon Kabat-Zinn, who had studied Buddhism, founded the Center for Mindfulness-Based Stress Reduction, and its outgrowth, the Center for Mindfulness in Medicine, Health Care, and Society, at the University of Massachusetts Medical School. Kabat-Zinn's clinic, and his later work in popularizing the practice of mindfulness, is largely responsible for bringing the concept into the mainstream of American thought. Kabat-Zinn's treatment approach, called mindfulness-based stress reduction (MBSR), asks patients to "draw on their inner resources and natural capacity to actively engage in caring for themselves and finding greater balance, ease, and peace of mind."[1]

In medicine, mindfulness is being utilized with both health care workers and patients. It is being taught at an increasing number of medical schools, including Harvard, Duke, and McGill, to help physicians relieve their own stress, and as a component of treatment for a number of stress-related illnesses, such as cardiovascular disease and diabetes. Psychologist Marsha M. Linehan designated mindfulness as a core concept in dialectical behavior therapy (DBT), a treatment now applied to several mental health issues. Other therapies using mindfulness, such as mindfulness-based cognitive therapy (MBCT), have been found effective in lessening the symptoms of anxiety and depression.

Corporations and educational institutions, too, have embraced mindfulness as a practice to help relieve stress and promote effective

---

1. Center for Mindfulness in Medicine, Health Care, and Society. "More than 30 Years of International Distinction." University of Massachusetts Medical School. Accessed April 22, 2014. http://www. umassmed.edu/cfm/index.aspx

decision making. Corporations such as Target and Google have offered employees mindfulness training, and business schools have added courses in mindfulness. Mindfulness training is also being included in a growing number of elementary and high school curriculums to promote a favorable atmosphere for teaching and learning.

Theories and Traditions Behind Mindfulness

Various approaches have been taken to help explain how the practice of mindfulness functions. Despite dramatically distinct viewpoints, ranging from traditional Buddhism to modern neuroscience, there are notable similarities.

Within classical Buddhist thought, the perceived need for things to be different than what they actually are is considered to be the cause of much suffering. Mindfulness assists the practitioner, through focused awareness of mental processes and physical sensations, to see the essential impermanence of observable facts or events. For Buddhists, this understanding promotes detachment, which takes the "emotional baggage" out of experience. Detachment is not seen as indifference, but rather as an important basis from which to cultivate acceptance and compassion toward ourselves and others.

In contemporary Western practice, including psychology, mindfulness is considered to be an approach that fosters increased awareness of mental processes and effective response to them. In this way, mindfulness training can improve decision making as well as our ability to adapt to different scenarios. When mindfulness researchers analyzed scores on both the Mindfulness Attention Awareness Scale (MAAS) and the Kentucky Inventory of Mindfulness Skills (KIMS), they found an association between the subjects' awareness, understanding, and acceptance of emotions and the subjects' ability to correct or improve unpleasant mood states.

Research on mindfulness training has shown its effectiveness in enhancing overall mental health and a sense of well-being. As an example in a clinical setting, awareness is thought to enable individuals being treated for depression to recognize depressive thought patterns early and thereby prevent depressive moods or relapse. In mindfulness-based cognitive therapy (MBCT), participants are taught to accept and observe common stressors without judgment, rather than reacting to them in what may be their usual pattern. The practice of mindfulness allows individuals to notice their automatic response process and to move from reaction to reflection.

Also associated with reduction in pain perception, it has been argued that the intentional use of mindful attention can be most therapeutic when that attention focuses on the concrete aspects of physical sensations rather than the emotions attached to them. Studies have shown that using mindfulness-based treatment to separate the sensations of pain from the emotional reactions to it causes the pain experience to decline.

Even more recent research on mindfulness has included not only the functional processes that are thought to be affected, but even the biology and neurology involved. For example, there is some evidence that the practice of mindfulness can actually enhance immunological functioning. The idea of neuroplasticity—the ability of the brain's pathways to grow, change, and adapt—is fairly new. Research has shown that mindfulness meditation, even for as brief a time as eight weeks, appears to make measurable changes in brain regions associated with memory, sense of self, empathy, and stress.

The insight that comes from a mindful perspective may have numerous psychological and behavioral benefits. For example, when automatic thought patterns are recognized and released, the rumination and obsessive thinking that can result in rigid emotional states and behaviors can be purposefully changed. Since mindfulness involves clarity of perspective about both internal and external phenomena, it can make us less reactive and better able to tolerate uncomfortable states and emotions. As we use mindfulness to monitor and manage our impulses to respond to experiences with habitual behavior (sometimes referred to as practicing executive attention), we may improve our self-control, planning, and decision-making capabilities, leading to a more balanced and healthful approach to living.

The Basics

To begin with, it is useful to think of mindfulness as encouraging *being*, rather than thinking. Being fully aware of your sensations, thoughts, and feelings may sound simple on the surface, but in reality, mindfulness requires regular exercise. If you are new to a mindfulness practice or need a refresher, this section will cover the roles of the essential elements, including the body, breath, and mind.

The Body

Although your experiences are filtered through your mind, your body plays a key role in the sensory sphere that delivers those experiences. Your physical being provides the tools with which you see, hear, touch, feel, and smell. And observing these physical sensations, without judgment, can help you both understand and respond differently to your body and mind.

Do not worry if you are somewhat reluctant to focus on your body or feel shy about its appearance. With a little practice, the mindfulness spotlight on the body will become easier and very rewarding. If by chance your experience of your body has been at times painful or distressing, do not hesitate to give it deliberate attention. Again, the payoff will soon outshine your initial reservations.

An intentional awareness of the body, central to the practice of mindfulness, can have powerful and positive effects for anyone. Through the practice of mindful attention to our bodies, we can better understand how we react to a host of sensory experiences. We can note the tension in the jaw if we are angry, experience the pain in the stomach if we are worried, feel the clenching of the fists if we are frustrated.

We can use our bodies to understand our patterns and then learn how to develop new ways to respond. We can relax rather than tense up, notice rather than resist, and treat each physical experience with a new perception.

The Breath

The breath, critical to life, is essential to mindfulness practice. We generally don't have to think about breathing—for most people it happens naturally. But with mindfulness, we can become fully aware of our breath. We can notice the process of our breathing as it occurs. We can observe the feeling at the nostrils with inhalation and exhalation, the experience of the breath as it passes through the throat and chest, the sensation of the rising and falling of the abdomen.

We can breathe without control, direction, or force. Yet when we are truly aware of our breath, we connect with the sensation of life as we breathe. We begin to concentrate. With focus on the breath, the thoughts, emotions, sensations, and sounds that can initially seem like distractions become objects of awareness themselves. Breath and mindfulness are inseparable.

The Mind

People sometimes think that meditating correctly means clearing all thoughts from the mind. But in mindfulness practice we don't try to stop or control our thoughts—we simply notice them. Our thoughts may shift from object to object, bring with them a variety of emotions, and seem as though they will never settle down. This "monkey mind" is not unusual, even in practiced meditators.

In mindfulness practice, we accept that our thoughts cannot be controlled by trying and our minds cannot be willed into submission. Rather, we observe and accept the paths our minds take. We understand that it's not by having thoughts but by getting *caught up* in those thoughts that we lose mindfulness. Rather, the process of mindfulness, paradoxically, lets our minds focus and frees our mental energy. It allows us to actually experience the present—as it happens.

When we practice mindfulness meditation, we should expect to have thoughts—often many thoughts. The thoughts are not an obstacle to meditation; they are an opportunity for us to deal with those thoughts in a new way. With our thoughts, as with our body and our breath, we simply practice attention and acceptance.

Our life is frittered away by detail.

—Henry David Thoreau, _Walden_

CHAPTER TWO

Why Practice Mindfulness?

The benefits of mindfulness have been affirmed by researchers, teachers, philosophers, and practitioners. Mindful living and mindful meditation can change our relationship to ourselves, to others, and to the world in which we live. Mindfulness can positively affect how we experience our bodies, how our minds function, how we respond to our emotions, and how we handle our relationships. Its benefits can extend to every aspect of our existence:

- **Mindfulness can increase our positive emotions and decrease negative ones.** It can counteract stress and even prevent depression.

- **Mindfulness can help us focus.** The practice of mindfulness increases the capacity for attention and develops our memory.

- **Mindfulness can improve problem-solving capabilities.** One study shows that after just a few weeks of mindfulness training, participants were better at exploring more strategies for problem solving.

- **Mindfulness can enhance mental resiliency.** Meditation can help a person withstand the emotional effects of traumatic events. Researchers found that mindfulness training seems to

NORTHERN PLAINS PUBLIC LIBRARY Ault, Colorado

provide individuals with a "mental shield," allowing them to stay alert and in the moment without becoming emotionally reactive.

- **Mindfulness builds the brain.** Investigators have found that mindfulness increases the density of gray matter and convolution or "gyrification" (the pattern and degree of cortical folding) in brain regions linked to learning, memory, emotion regulation, and empathy. It may also contribute to faster information processing, higher intelligence, and less age-related brain shrinkage.

- **Mindfulness can lessen the experience of physical pain.** People who regularly meditate find pain less distressing and experience less pain sensitivity.

- **Mindfulness can improve our overall health.** In one study, researchers found that after just eight weeks of training, practicing mindfulness meditation boosted the body's immune system, increasing its ability to fight off illness.

- **Mindfulness can improve relationships.** The receptive attentiveness that characterizes mindfulness may enhance an individual's ability to notice and be interested in their partner's thoughts, emotions, and well-being.

- **Mindfulness fosters compassion and altruism.**

Modern Life and Mindfulness

Though the practice of mindfulness meditation has existed for millennia, modern conditions underscore the need for a way to handle pressures and improve our daily lives. The pattern of fragmented living that is characteristic of the digital age can rob us of health, joy, and peace of mind. Despite all the information we can access and all the methods of continuous communication we use, we may often feel uncertain, distracted, and worried—connected to everything but ourselves. We're always thinking, but may often feel out of focus. We may be overwhelmed by anxiety and negativity, distressed with concerns about the future or regrets about the past. Even when it seems like everything is objectively fine, we may feel dissatisfied and unable to experience the happiness that somehow is just out of our grasp. In other words, we may live our lives on autopilot, reacting to events and emotions rather than making considered choices. We're always on, but we're not always present.

The practice of mindfulness provides an antidote to the steady stresses of modern living. When we are able to focus our consciousness so that we can live our lives fully in the present, when we allow ourselves to *be* rather than always having to *do*, we can counteract some of the pressures that assault our bodies, minds, and spirits. Through the practice of mindfulness, we can find greater balance and peace. We can learn how to *be here now*.

The Mindfulness Journal

One useful tool in the practice of mindfulness is keeping a mindfulness journal. The process of writing in a journal helps us begin the shift from connecting to the outside world to connecting to ourselves. We move from assessing and evaluating each idea and thought to simply allowing thoughts to flow and observing what comes up.

By writing in your mindfulness journal, you are already moving toward the practice of mindfulness. Observing your thoughts without judgment, experiencing your feelings at that moment, paying attention—this is the essence of mindfulness. But as simple as it sounds, you'll probably notice that it's not so easy. And, of course, you'll want to do something about that. You'll want to do it right. You'll want to "fix" it. You'll want to be good at mindfulness. But keep in mind that the paradox of mindfulness practice is that it all starts with—and is continued by—letting go of the need to improve and change things.

Perhaps you worry that what you are writing in your journal is too negative and focuses on all the "wrong" reasons for practicing mindfulness. Or perhaps you find yourself writing about something completely different than the prompt suggested. Or you realize that you aren't actually writing down your thoughts as they come, but are selecting some thoughts and ignoring others. No matter what happens, noticing it is all part of the practice of mindfulness.

TIP *Carry your mindfulness journal with you and use it frequently to write—using stream of consciousness—about what you are experiencing at that moment.*

Cultivating awareness doesn't require changing what your thoughts are, but simply paying attention to them, whatever they may be. And the further paradox of mindfulness practice is that this observation and acceptance of what is happening in the moment doesn't mean that you can't have a goal of longer-term change. Quite the contrary, in fact. You may want to relieve stress or anxiety, manage pain differently, or find greater satisfaction in life through the practice of mindfulness—the key is that while knowing what you want to achieve, the focus of your mindfulness practice should be on the awareness of these thoughts in the moment, not on changing them.

Over time, by remaining present with whatever arises, something can begin to happen. You may notice a part of yourself that can experience the ebb and flow of both pleasant and unpleasant thoughts with less judgment and less stress. By not trying to change your thoughts, mindfulness actually changes your relationship to them. This new awareness and clarity allows space for making choices, rather than reacting to circumstances.

EXERCISE Mindfulness Journal

Begin your mindfulness journal with the same intention that is at the core of all mindfulness practice: to stay present and fully aware. *As you commence your* practice, *it may help to find a location where you can be without distraction, even if just for a few minutes. Start with a blank journal or a blank page and follow a few simple steps:*

1. *Decide how much time you will spend writing your entry. This can be one minute, twenty minutes, one hour—you decide each time you're about to write.*

2. *Choose a prompt. This can be a question, a word, an image— anything you want to use to inspire your writing.*

3. *Write! Just put your pen on the paper or your fingers on the keyboard and begin to write. Don't edit, don't censor, don't hesitate, don't judge—just write. Let your thoughts rise up and flow onto the blank page. This "stream-of-consciousness" writing allows you to access a part of you that is beyond the conscious self-critical voice and tune into your experience of the moment.*

JOURNAL PROMPT *For the first entry in your mindfulness journal, consider the question "Why have I decided to try a mindfulness practice?"*

As you begin, remember that the most essential part of mindfulness practice is just that: practice. Your mindfulness journal can be a tool to help you focus and free yourself from the clamoring demands of daily life. So take some time each day—even if just briefly—and write about what you're feeling in that moment with attention, awareness, and acceptance.

How Mindfulness Helps

Each of us begins mindfulness practice with our own individual motivation. For example, we may want to reduce stress, manage pain, relieve anxiety or depression, think more positively, sleep better, focus more, or derive greater satisfaction from our work or our relationships. Although it is important to understand that practicing mindfulness is not about achieving goals, there are certain issues that the practice of mindfulness can help us recognize and deal with differently and more confidently.

Stress

We may say, "I can't take any more stress," or "This stress is really getting to me." But what are we actually talking about? We experience stress when, sensing a threat, primitive parts of the brain are triggered into a fight-or-flight response. Our system has automatic physiological reactions, including increased heart rate, muscle tension, blood pressure, and focus. This heightened state of arousal can continue until something—such as a removal of the threat—allows the body to return to a resting state.

The fight-or-flight response was well adapted to the experience of ancient cave dwellers threatened by saber-toothed tigers, but it presents problems in modern life. Although we may also face some life-threatening crises and fight-or-flight can still help protect us, most of the dangers we perceive are not immediate physical threats. We may face the danger of losing our job, our partner, or a promotion. We may fear not meeting a deadline, not being a good parent, or not being appreciated for our efforts. Our stresses are often chronic, and so we remain in a heightened state of arousal. Our bodies and minds never have the opportunity to calm down. In other words, the tigers never go away.

This chronic stress can have serious consequences for our mental and physical well-being. Fight-or-flight doesn't work well for ongoing stressful experiences when there is no time for rest and recovery. Chronic stress can negatively impact cognitive functioning, regulation of emotions, physical health, and a sense of well-being, both in the short and long term.

Mindfulness allows us to step back from the thoughts and feelings we have in response to stress—and to realize that those thoughts and feelings, in themselves, have no inherent power over us. We often get caught up in reviewing past problems, feel overwhelmed by anxiety about the future, and exist in an ongoing state of stress. When we connect with the present moment instead—calmly observing and accepting our thoughts, emotions, and sensations—we are better able to handle them. We can come down from our heightened fight-or-flight state.

There is a steadily developing body of evidence demonstrating the beneficial effect of mindfulness practice on stress reduction. More than two decades of research indicate that the majority of people who complete mindfulness training report a greater ability to cope more effectively with both short- and long-term stressful situations. Studies of cognitive processes indicate that mindfulness meditation increases awareness and the creation of alternatives to automatic behavior. This reduces the stress response by allowing conscious thoughts to move from uncontrollable past or future scenarios to an acceptance of current experience.

Neurological studies have also shown mindfulness practice to be associated with specific changes in the brain that can result in improved stress management. Mindfulness lessens activity in the amygdala, a part of the brain that is responsible for evaluating threats. This reduces the likelihood of overreaction and improves our capacity to problem-solve effectively. The automatic need for fight-or-flight is diminished by the ability to see and accept.

Pain

Historically, the intensity of pain was thought to be directly related to the degree of injury to the body; if different people had the same physical damage, then it was assumed that they would suffer from the same amount of pain. Now, it is clear that pain is a more complex phenomenon. The brain interprets the sensation before it is consciously felt. Pain then becomes a fusion of thought and sensation. The thoughts that are attached to the sensation can have a dramatic effect on the experience of the pain.

We experience suffering on two levels. First there are the unpleasant sensations that are sent to the brain from the nerves responding to an injury or ongoing physical damage or illness. Then all the associated thoughts, feelings, emotions, and memories are overlaid on the initial sensations. The combination of these two levels of experience results in our actual suffering. Understanding how feelings of pain occur is critical to pain management through mindfulness practice. With mindfulness, we can observe the different elements of pain and greatly reduce suffering and distress. This does not in any way suggest that pain is not real. It exists and can seem overwhelming. But understanding how the mind mediates the experience of pain helps us diminish its power and lessen the suffering we feel.

When Jon Kabat-Zinn founded the Stress Reduction Clinic at the University of Massachusetts Medical School, he expected that patients would be able to transform their relationship to pain using mindfulness meditation. He theorized that separating the actual sensations of pain from the emotional reactions to it would help patients realize that at least part of their suffering was the result of emotions, and not just the sensations themselves. Therefore, a reappraisal of reactions could decrease a patient's suffering even if the physical source of the pain did not go away.

Kabat-Zinn's theories were validated by research on mindfulness meditation and pain experience. Decreases in suffering in chronic pain patients who practiced mindfulness meditation were associated with increased perceived control over pain and reduced reactivity to distressing thoughts and emotions. In the laboratory, research participants reported less distress and greater tolerance of acute pain when they were practicing mindfulness, compared to people who were not meditating.

Now scientists are also using brain imaging to discover how we process the emotional aspects of pain while meditating. The various data indicate that meditation involves multiple brain mechanisms that can alter our individual experience of pain.

With mindfulness practice, we can:

- Allow ourselves to notice the pain before it overwhelms us, and pace activity accordingly
- Hinder the cycle of pain, anxiety, depression, and exhaustion that contributes to suffering
- Soothe the perception of pain by replacing it with a sense of calm

Depression and Anxiety

Most of us have felt anxious or depressed at one time or another because of life circumstances: losing a job, the death of a loved one, or even giving a presentation or taking a test. Difficult situations, large and small, can lead us to feel sad, scared, nervous, or worried. These are normal reactions to stress.

Sometimes, though, these feelings become a person's primary experience of life and occur daily, or very frequently, for no clear reason. Such feelings make it difficult to carry on with normal, everyday functioning, sometimes leading to an anxiety disorder, a depressive disorder, or both. Mindfulness training can help with common anxiety and sadness, and can be an important part of the treatment plan if these issues become serious clinical conditions.

When experiencing anxiety, you may notice physical symptoms, such as a rapid heartbeat, shakiness, sweating, nausea, or a dry mouth. You may feel fearful, worried, and distracted. It's typical to want to escape from whatever it is that's making you feel that way.

Depressed individuals may spend long periods of time thinking about problems, rehashing events of the day, and ruminating over difficulties. This leads to increased negative thoughts, poor problem solving, difficulty initiating any activity, impaired concentration, and increased experience of stress.

Some mental health theorists consider anxiety and depression to be two sides of the same coin. Individuals who are vulnerable to both conditions often share the experience of overestimating the risk of a given situation and underestimating their ability to cope with it. Both depressed and anxious individuals may think, for example, *I'll never do well on this interview, so I won't get this job,* as well as *I'll really go under if I don't get this job.* In addition, depressed and anxious individuals may cope by avoiding what they fear rather than developing skills to handle uncomfortable situations. Research indicates that those who are clinically depressed and anxious may experience over-reactivity of the stress-response system, sending the emotional centers of the brain, including the alarm center in the amygdala, into overdrive.

Research provides evidence that mindfulness meditation may be as effective as antidepressants at providing relief from some anxiety and depression symptoms. Findings also indicate that mindfulness meditation increases positive emotions and decreases worry and negativity, reducing self-reported anxiety and depression. Participants in one study, when exposed to sad or unnerving stimuli, displayed distinctly different neural responses than they did before their mindfulness training. These findings all suggest that mindfulness meditation shifts our ability to use emotion-regulation strategies so we can experience emotion selectively, and that those emotions may be processed differently in the brain.

Mindfulness practice helps us develop a whole new relationship with our thoughts. It guides us to a state of balance, where we can allow ourselves to feel everything without being overwhelmed by it. The thoughts don't have to change. They can still have the same worrisome content: *This will never work . . . Nobody cares.* But with mindfulness practice, we begin to see that these thoughts are simply that—thoughts. We no longer have to judge them, feel compelled to act upon them, or indeed do anything much about them. They merely arise in our mind and then dissolve. They no longer have the power to control us. Avoidance repertoires, which may cause us to cope with depression or anxiety by avoiding what we believe to be the cause of our distress, can be observed, accepted, and allowed to melt away. The negative reinforcement that supports the avoidance—*I can't do that,* or *I can't talk to him*—can be replaced by more effective problem-solving capabilities and greater peace of mind.

Negative Thought Patterns

Often based on automatic ways of responding, negative thought patterns sometimes play over and over in our heads, unchallenged, for years. These habitual scripts can take many forms, including the following:

- **Incessant worry.** One type of negative thinking is imagining or expecting that bad things will happen or that nothing good will ever happen. *I'll never find someone to love me,* or *I'm never going to pass my exams.*

- **Constant criticism.** Another negative thought pattern is constant criticism of yourself and others. You may be very harsh on yourself, focusing on all of your weaknesses and perceived flaws, or only see the flaws in others. For example, *I'm lousy at this job,* or *My boss is a real jerk.* When these critical habits extend to those close to us, it can put a real strain on relationships.

- **Regret and guilt.** Ruminating on past mistakes is a debilitating form of negativity. Playing "bad" choices and "wrong" behavior over and over results in chronic feelings of guilt and worthlessness.

- **Catastrophizing.** This negative thought process involves imagining the worst-case scenario or outcome of a stressful event or experience, such as worrying about a cut leading to an infection and then requiring an amputation.

- **Focusing on problems.** In this type of negative thinking, your attention becomes fixated on and exaggerates the negative aspects of your life, and you may often minimize what is going well. You might do very well on a test, but instead of feeling satisfied with your effort, you instead think: *Why did I get that question wrong? What a stupid mistake.*

- **Dissatisfaction.** Obsessively focusing on all the things you want but do not have is another negative thought pattern. Perceiving desires as needs short-circuits the joys in life and gives external objects the power to control happiness.

- **Labeling.** This habit creates generalizations about ourselves and others and interferes with real understanding. Thinking *I'm a loser,* interferes with our ability to connect to our strengths and accomplish our goals.

Negative thinking slips into our minds before we are consciously aware of it and becomes one of our strongest habit patterns. We generate negative thoughts so automatically that it's easy to forget we have any other choice. Negative thought patterns can hold us captive. We may try different ways to free ourselves of negative thoughts—distraction, diversions, self-control—and instead we end up criticizing ourselves for still being submerged in negativity. Resisting the negative thought will often backfire—you'll usually reinforce it and make it even worse. The more you follow the pathway of negativity, the stronger the pattern becomes.

Mindfulness meditation can help free us from the prison of negativity and connect us with our real experience. The first step in the struggle with negative thinking is to recognize that our thoughts are merely thoughts. Mindfulness helps us see our thought patterns more clearly and recognize when we are moving into negativity. Awareness and acceptance can help us let things go before negative thoughts capture us. Mindfulness can help us halt the escalation of negative thinking by focusing on the present moment rather than ruminating on the past or future.

With mindfulness, we develop a willingness to face our challenging emotions and deal with pain. By becoming a curious observer of our own experience, we can notice our distress, but we don't have to fight it or conquer it. Instead, we can develop flexibility in our responses that enables us to turn down the volume on negativity. We can allow our difficult thoughts and feelings to come and go, and we can see them from a different perspective, a perspective that no longer controls us.

Sleep

Sleep disorder is another area in which mindfulness appears to be particularly useful. Sleep disturbance is a common problem; nearly seventy-five percent of American adults report having at least one type of sleep problem a few nights a week or more. Insomnia is linked to serious health conditions, including heart disease, diabetes complications, depression, and even premature death.

Every day, our bodies experience alternating cycles of activity, sleep, temperature variation, hormone secretion, and other biological functions. But sleep disturbance can alter these normal rhythms. Individuals who suffer from chronic insomnia will often describe their condition as a vicious cycle: They try harder and harder to go to sleep or get back to sleep. They feel stuck between feeling sleepy and wakeful, and are overwhelmed by the desire to get more nighttime rest and avoid daytime fatigue.

When you lie down at night, ideally your mind should be able to turn off all the internal noise and allow the brain waves to follow the natural architecture of sleep, giving the body time to regenerate. If, however, your mind remains in an alert state, if you continue to actively review the past day and preview the next, the mind can't disengage and the body can't relax and rest.

Mindfulness has been proven to reduce or eliminate this hyperaroused state, helping restore the balance within and allowing us to rest. Mindfulness-based treatments for insomnia hypothesize that in order for us to sleep, our minds must experience cognitive deactivation. This means less conscious information processing as compared with daytime functioning, and more nonjudgmental acceptance of physiological and mental processes as they are occurring.

A preliminary study has been conducted on mindfulness-based therapy for insomnia (MBT-I). Participants were taught to respond to sleep disturbance with mindfulness skills rather than react automatically by increasing effort to rest. They used awareness of internal cues for sleep and recognition of reactive tendencies to make changes in both their relationship to sleep and their behaviors likely to promote sleep. Half of the participants experienced a reduction in total wake time, and all but two participants scored below the cutoff for clinically significant insomnia on the Insomnia Severity Index. In addition, the mindfulness-based therapy resulted in significant reductions in wakefulness before bedtime, effort to sleep, and dysfunctional sleep-related thoughts.

A controlled clinical trial of mindfulness-based stress reduction resulted in some interesting outcomes related to sleep. People suffering from chronic insomnia who participated in this program had results equivalent to another group who used pharmaceutical sleep aids.

Mindfulness teaches us that focusing on trying to get to sleep may interfere with achieving it, and, paradoxically, letting go of the effort may help us sleep.

TIP *For more on mindfulness and sleep, see page 78.*

Focus

Multitasking is often promoted as a sought-after skill, and concentration on a single task has been viewed as underproductive. However, there is growing evidence that the more we take on, the less we are able to accomplish. Our minds have become used to wandering from task to task, and even at crucial moments, we can become sidetracked by a variety of distractions: a ticking clock, thoughts about the next meal, or worries about events completely unrelated to the job at hand.

Mindfulness and mindfulness meditation practices can help us find stillness in the midst of multiple obligations and distractions. When we feel pressure and stress, our attention begins to fade away. Our thoughts may wander. We want to focus on one thing, but can't seem to concentrate. A potent antidote to this lack of focus, mindfulness brings our balanced and full attention to whatever is at hand —enjoying breakfast, giving a presentation, meeting with friends.

It reminds us to notice when we are seduced by distractions and not attending to the present moment. Mindfulness strengthens our ability to track our attention and move it back to what we are doing right then, allowing us to single-task and ultimately accomplish more.

Investigators found that students who received mindfulness training improved their reading comprehension scores on standardized tests, increased their working memory capacity, and experienced a decrease in distracting thoughts. Other studies have found similar results, with mindfulness meditation demonstrating improvements in short-term memory and the ability to resist distractions.

Life Satisfaction

Mindfulness cultivates attitudes and behaviors that encourage life satisfaction. It makes the pleasures of life easier to notice and enjoy, helps us become more committed to activities in the moment, and promotes a greater capacity to deal with difficult life challenges. Mindfulness has been associated with reduction in stress, better pain management, improved relief of anxiety and depression, more positive thinking, better sleep, and clearer focus—all of which lead to greater overall satisfaction. It helps us control distractions so we can get more done and feel good about it, and it allows us to reduce our automatic thinking; and research has shown a corollary link to life satisfaction. Mindfulness brings us into closer contact with life by helping us avoid the narratives that are *about* life yet tend to pull us away from the direct experience of it.

Recent studies indicate that the specific benefits of mindfulness can also help us feel greater satisfaction in our work, our relationships, and life in general. Participants in a study who practiced mindfulness techniques for a brief period each day over a period of three weeks reported significant reductions in stress, along with increases in life satisfaction and positive relations with others.

It's possible that the receptive attention that is central to mindfulness might enhance our ability to pay attention to others and to be more fully aware of emotional tones as well as nonverbal cues.

Learning to be present in the moment allows us to be more flexible and resilient, and less stubborn and resistant. Observing our thoughts without being attached to them, and accepting them without trying to change them, can facilitate equanimity, ease, and a sense of well-being that is stable and not dependent on life circumstances.

Core Components of a Mindfulness Practice

Although the practice of mindfulness can have many positive results, such as relaxation and mood management, mindfulness approaches are generally considered a form of mental training. The benefits of this training are not goals to be achieved. Rather, they occur naturally as a corollary of the practice itself.

Two important elements are at the core of mindfulness practice:

- **Being present in the moment.** This requires practice, primarily through mindfulness meditation. It can also be nurtured through other methods, such as using a mindfulness journal, bringing mindfulness to everyday events, or engaging in mindfulness activities. Being present sounds easy, but even for experienced practitioners it requires regular exercise to maintain. Our minds are skilled in creating worries about tomorrow, criticizing yesterday's mistakes, and following the numerous paths that can take us away from the moment we are in.

  Being present means just that. Feeling your feelings as they come up. Experiencing your sensations as they occur. Noticing your thoughts as they come into your consciousness.

  Being present means being here now.

■   **Nonjudgmental acceptance of our experience.** This requires
    the ability to embrace whatever we encounter in the present
    moment and let it be.

    Acceptance means being able to notice our thoughts, feelings,
    and sensations without immediately assigning a particular
    meaning or attaching a judgment to them. It allows us to be
    less disturbed by unpleasant thoughts and less reactive to
    unpleasant experiences.

Mindfulness can help us begin to recognize the patterns of
the mind that have developed beyond our customary consciousness, and respond to life in new ways rather than with old habits.
Maintaining an open and curious attitude toward our experiences
as they occur allows us to see everything from a new perspective, as
if we are encountering it for the first time.

PART TWO

The Practice of Mindfulness

We shape our tools and afterwards our tools shape us.

—Marshall McLuhan

CHAPTER THREE

Creating the Environment

Although mindfulness can actually be practiced anytime and anywhere, some conditions can support and enhance it. This can be particularly helpful when you're just beginning to train your mind in its methods.

Getting Started

As you know by this point, the practice of mindfulness meditation is central to learning and supporting the overall practice of mindfulness. When you decide to begin mindfulness meditation, it is helpful to prepare by setting aside time and space for the practice, assembling any aids that might be useful, and following certain procedures that can strengthen the result.

A Supportive Environment

You can meditate anywhere you feel like—in a garden, at work, or even at the airport waiting for a flight. However, although having a meditation area is not mandatory in order to practice successfully, creating the right physical environment can make it easier to practice. It helps to meditate regularly in the same location, where distractions are minimized and the atmosphere is calm. If possible, select a room or corner in your home that can be dedicated to your mindfulness meditation. If you have a room with a peaceful view, so much the better. You may also use this room for another purpose, so consider selecting a corner of it for your practice. If you need to practice in a location that does not provide a feeling of serenity, you may want to add an object, such as a painting or poster, that promotes this atmosphere.

Ensuring that your meditation space is neat, clean, and well ventilated is also helpful in encouraging your practice. Your meditation setting should allow you to focus. Even the colors and lighting can be important in making it more likely for you to concentrate on your meditation. Some people prefer light colors, finding dark or bright shades distracting. Some prefer dim lights, while others like more lighting. The specific details can be of your own choosing—just make your selections thoughtfully and tailor them to your needs. You may choose to include some items that provide you with a calm feeling. Even a small altar or candles may work as an anchor for your practice. But it is not necessary to introduce any particular items into this special space. What is most important is what is *not* there.

Your meditation spot should not include anything that would be distracting, such as a TV screen. It should not have pictures or mementos that foster strong emotions like anger, jealousy, or sadness. It should not be noisy or easily open to disturbance. Turn your phone off (or keep it on low and in another location) so you can actually disconnect from your daily pulls and pressures. You can even set up your meditation space facing a blank wall, as long as that allows you to create an atmosphere that you find conducive to your practice.

Meditating in a space identified for that purpose helps remind you of what you're doing. It helps you attend to the practice of mindfulness by saying, "This place is meant for mindfulness."

TIP *You can even create a small space at your work desk to use for*
your meditation. Make sure that the area is clean and empty of any
distracting objects before you begin your practice. You may choose to
put up a few calming images if you like. Turn your phone to silent mode,
and shut down your computer for a few minutes while you meditate.

A Designated Seat and a Balanced Posture

When choosing where to sit as you meditate, it is better to avoid
meditating directly on the floor, which can be uncomfortable, or on a
bed, which is associated with sleep and can create some confusion in
your mind about what you're doing. When you practice mindfulness
meditation, you don't want to experience discomfort or encourage
sleepiness. You may choose a soft yoga mat with a pillow that allows
you to sit easily or a chair with a proper backrest. The most important
thing is that you are comfortable and focused while meditating.

If you're using a chair, you should sit up straight with your
feet easily touching the floor. If you decide to sit on a pillow or a
folded blanket, sit with your legs loosely crossed and your hands
resting on your thighs. An ideal meditative position evokes a feeling of stability and strength.

The best posture for meditating may feel unfamiliar at first,
but should still be comfortable and relaxed. Your spine should be
upright and erect, maintaining its natural curve; your shoulders
and hips should be level, but not rigid or strained. Having a straight
spine helps your breathing be more relaxed and enhances alert-
ness. This posture should help you stay both calm and aware. As
you meditate, your eyes may be gently closed. If you prefer them
to remain open, you can gaze slightly downward at a point four to
six feet in front of you. Your gaze shouldn't be too tightly focused.
Do not stare or do anything special with your gaze; just let it rest
where you've set it. Either of these eye positions will help minimize
distractions as you continue your practice. When you sit down to

meditate, the first thing to do is to fully inhabit your body. This means you should begin with a sense of your body—feel where it is, notice how it feels. Spend some time experiencing your body. Be there with it. This may, in fact, be your entire meditation. Whatever the length of your meditation, always spend some time settling into your posture at the beginning.

A Designated Time and Length

Daily meditation is ideal for mindfulness practice. It is helpful to pick a time for practice each day, since you're more likely to meditate if you make an appointment with yourself to do it.

In theory, the best times for meditating are in the early morning, at sunset, or late in the evening. But the time you choose should suit your daily routines and also be accommodating to anyone you live with. If you're scheduling your meditation time around the schedule of others in your household, you may want to consider when their usual activities will provide you with the most undisturbed time. Most important, the time should work for you and encourage you to meditate regularly.

Once you have chosen a preferred time, allow yourself to be flexible and experiment with it. You may consider different times for different reasons:

- **Early morning.** Meditating first thing in the morning can set the tone for the entire day. Like eating a healthy breakfast and brushing your teeth, making meditation part of your daily morning routine can help it become a regular part of how you live your life.

- **Lunchtime.** Midday meditation can help you break from a stressful routine and remind you to incorporate your mindfulness practice into your day. It can help you build awareness as you experience your daily life and notice where you spend much of your time.

- **Early evening.** For some, early evening marks the boundary between work and home; for others, it's a boundary between time spent caring for others and time for oneself; and for still others, it's simply a time when most of the day's activities are winding down. It's often a good time for mindfulness meditation because focusing on the present moment can help us let go of many of the concerns of the day and view experiences with a new perspective.

- **Late evening.** This is often a convenient time for meditation, but it's important that any late-evening mindfulness meditation not be part of a bedtime ritual. If this is the time that works for you, then you should meditate at least an hour before you plan to go to sleep, so that you're not too tired to meditate effectively. The end of a very long day can be a tempting time to skip meditation. So if you do feel tired, you might just take a few moments to experience your breath and reinforce your mindfulness meditation intention.

If you must miss a scheduled meditation time, do not merely change the meditation time that day. First acknowledge that this is your meditation time, but you will not be keeping your appointment that day. Just for a moment, pause and remember your intention to meditate. Then you can do your meditation at a later time. This pause will help solidify your commitment and further support your practice of awareness. For most people's beginning meditation practice, it may be best to cultivate a sincere attitude of commitment to specific times, with a little flexibility toward changing events.

The duration of your meditation practice is also up to you. You can decide to meditate for two minutes, five minutes, thirty minutes—it's your choice. For beginners, a frequent recommendation is to meditate each day for ten to twenty minutes. This allows time to settle into your body; notice your thoughts, feelings, and sensations; and practice letting them go. It provides enough time for an extended period of exercising mindfulness, but not so much time that your frustration with your efforts will overwhelm you.

You may choose instead to begin with much shorter periods of mindfulness meditation, gradually building up your ability to focus on the present and slowly acquiring the ability to experience the moment with nonjudgmental acceptance. Brief meditations can be done throughout the day, reinforcing your practice and developing your mindfulness skills. Even meditating for a few moments can help you connect to yourself.

A Meditation Anchor

While we are meditating, it is inevitable that we will periodically become lost in our thoughts or feelings. When we are distracted or having difficulty noticing without evaluating, a meditation anchor can help focus our attention and bring it back to a state of mindfulness.

Meditation anchors can be many things—objects, parts of the body, words, or even your breath.

- **Objects.** You can select any physical object as an anchor for your drifting mind. It can be a candle, an image, or even a rock. The important thing is that it is not associated with any powerful emotions or memories and that it encourages a feeling of calm. Using an object as an anchor is best if you prefer to keep your eyes open during meditation. The object should be placed where your gaze would naturally fall during your practice—below you and about six feet in front of where you're sitting.

- **Parts of the body.** A meditation anchor does not have to be separate from you. For example, you can use a part of your body, such as your hand. As your mind begins to wander, concentrate on your hand, noticing the sensations you are experiencing and examining its qualities, the folds of your skin, the length of your fingers, the color of your palm. One advantage of choosing a body part is that you'll have your object of focus with you all the time, whenever you want to use it.

- **Words.** A word, phrase, or sound used to aid concentration is called a *mantra*. In Eastern practices, mantras were traditionally given to meditation students by their teachers and served as reminders of important thoughts or concepts. But the content of a mantra is not the critical element. A mantra, whatever its content, has two essential functions: (1) it helps to replace the stream of wandering thoughts with a focus; and (2) it becomes associated in your mind with a calm state and can be used at various times, even when you're not meditating, to help you relax.

  You can use any word or phrase as your mantra. You can select a traditional mantra, such as the Hindu word *om*; you can use a word or phrase that is uplifting, like "joy" or "peace on earth"; or you can use a mantra that is simply a repeated phrase, such as "up and down" or "one, two." It can even just be a meaningless sound that you find calming.

  You can repeat your mantra aloud or silently focus on the sound it makes in your mind. As you become more practiced, you can apply this sound to bring you back to the present during your meditation or at any time during the day.

- **Breath.** The breath is an essential part of any mindfulness meditation. One of its functions is as an anchor. Begin your mindfulness practice by developing a sense of your body and your surroundings, and then begin to notice your breathing. Your breath should come naturally. It should not be forced or pressured. Don't try to change it. Let your attention rest on the breath as you inhale and exhale in a natural rhythm. Experience your breath and be aware of it, one breath at a time.

TIP *When you use your breath as an anchor, you might find that mentally counting each breath you take helps to maintain your focus. If you get entangled in thoughts as you count (and you will), just notice it and begin again.*

Whatever you decide to use as an anchor for your meditation, when you find your mind wandering, simply bring it back to the anchor, relaxing the body and returning your attention to the present moment.

Helpful Tools

There are some items that have been designed for meditation practice. You might find it helpful to use a few of these tools.

- **Meditation cushion.** There are a number of different traditional meditation cushions that can help you find a comfortable position as you practice. A *gomden* is a firm, rectangular cushion that is used worldwide to help practitioners maintain their seated pose while meditating. A *zafu* is the dense, round cushion traditionally used in Zen meditation. A *zabuton* mat, frequently used in Japanese meditation centers, may be placed under your cushion to make your feet and legs more comfortable.

- **Meditation bench.** These generally wooden constructions are designed to help practitioners achieve the most useful meditation posture. Benches are higher than cushions and usually slightly tilted to facilitate a straight-back, cross-legged posture. *Seiza* benches are specifically fashioned to be used with the kneeling meditation position used in Japanese Zen meditation.

- **Pillow or chair.** Although the many posture supports available are designed to make your meditation practice more comfortable and relaxed, it isn't necessary to purchase any specific equipment in order to achieve an optimal meditation posture. You can place a pillow or folded blanket on a mat on the floor to help maintain your body in a comfortable pose. Or you can sit on a chair that provides back support (perhaps using an additional cushion here, as well), with your feet on the ground. It's not important what you use, but what it accomplishes: a comfortable, relaxed upright pose.

- **Meditation clothing.** While mindfulness meditation does not require any particular attire, you can purchase specific clothing intended for meditation, including shawls, tops, and pants. However, you can meditate productively in anything that is easy to wear and useful in maintaining a comfortable body temperature.

- **Timer.** A timer can let you know when your meditation practice has been completed without the distraction of regularly checking a clock. Timers come in many forms. Some are devices that indicate completion by sounding an actual or electronic gong. You can also download silent audio files of different lengths that have a gong to signal the beginning of your practice and several gongs to indicate the end. Some timers are apps for your cell phone that allow you to configure the specific sound you want to use to delineate the end of your meditation session. Most also offer a vibrate option so that no sound is necessary to signal when your meditation is done. No special device is necessary, however. If you are timing your meditation, a simple clock or phone alarm can be used to tell you when the time for meditation is over.

- **Meditation audio.** Many meditation audios are available as downloadable files, apps, or CDs. These can provide guidance in mindfulness practice by giving step-by-step instructions for various exercises as you do them. It may be helpful not to have to try to remember how to do the next stage of the practice you're using for that day's meditation. But since mindfulness requires practice and not perfection, the important thing is not the steps you follow, but the attention you use.

Using music audio during mindfulness meditation can be distracting and usually is not recommended. However, some people find a recording of sounds from nature, replicating the outdoors, helpful to their meditation practice.

Mindfulness Anytime, Anywhere

You might imagine or even have the luxury of a meditation room dedicated to mindfulness practice. Upon entering, you would know that you were about to enhance your mindfulness skills. Such a room would provide the serenity and freedom from external distraction to assist you in focused meditation. It would be light and airy and contain all the objects you would want to use in your meditation practice—a comfortable cushion or chair, perhaps a candle to help you focus, a timer to let you know when your meditation session is complete.

Although it is helpful to have environmental supports for your mindfulness practice, in reality all you need are your body, your breath, and your mind. Everything else might be useful in some way—to make you more comfortable and relaxed, or make it easier for you to concentrate your attention, or more likely for you to meditate regularly—but such elements are not essential to your mindfulness practice.

The biggest hurdle may appear to be time. It never seems as though we have the time to get everything done, let alone to practice mindfulness. How can we spare a half hour to meditate?

Well, don't. Use whatever time you have available—five minutes, twenty minutes, even one minute. You can take brief periods for mindfulness meditation exercises—focusing, for example, on your breath. You can work mindfulness into your daily life in an informal way. When you're waiting for the elevator or walking to your car, you can simply be mindful of your thoughts, emotions, and body sensations. The more you practice mindfulness, the more likely it is to be available to you with less effort. It is a skill that can be learned. You already have the capacity for mindfulness. You merely have to exercise it.

TIP *You can use your journal for a mindful pause. At any point during the day, open your journal, turn your attention inward, and use stream-of-consciousness writing to record a thought about your mindfulness practice or respond to a prompt.*

JOURNAL PROMPT *"What am I feeling right now, in this moment?"*

Just as you can practice mindfulness anytime, for any length of time, you can also practice it anywhere. You can be mindful while you eat your breakfast, noticing the taste, texture, and smell of everything you're eating, chewing slowly, swallowing thoughtfully. You can pause before you get in line at the store and get in touch with your experience at that moment. Notice what you see, hear, and feel. Become aware of your emotional state as you feel it. Do you feel bored, stressed, excited? Just notice the emotion without judgment or evaluation. You can walk with mindfulness, feeling your feet as they contact the ground. Keep your attention on the sensations of your body as you walk, and allow yourself to notice the experience in great detail.

Wherever and whenever you can practice mindfulness, do. You need nothing but your intention. Remember, you're training your mind to function in a new way. And like any new skill, it requires practice. And more practice. And even more practice.

_____

*Try looking at your mind as a wayward puppy that you
are trying to paper train.... You just keep bringing it
back to the newspaper. So I keep trying gently to bring
my mind back to what is really there to be seen, maybe
to be seen and noted with a kind of reverence.*

—Anne Lamott, *Bird by Bird*

CHAPTER FOUR

A First Meditation

Each meditation session is a journey of discovery. It does not have a destination; it does not have a goal. It's a process through which we learn more about who we are and how we function. Our lives are spent developing mental habits that are the opposite of mindfulness. Learning a new way to be, disentangling ourselves from our ingrained behaviors and thought patterns, and letting go of the stories we tell about our feelings and experiences require a powerful strategy.

The idea of the strategy itself, mindfulness meditation, is very simple. With mindfulness meditation, we give our full awareness to our sensations, emotions, and thoughts—and we accept those experiences without judgment. As you may be discovering, the practice of that strategy, however, is not as easy as it sounds. But you can do it—and the rewards will greatly justify your efforts.

Just as we must regularly exercise physically in order to develop new muscle strength, we must regularly practice mindfulness in order to develop new thought patterns. We should set aside the time and space to give our practice the opportunity to thrive. We should make a sincere commitment, starting in this moment, to live life mindfully.

As you plan to begin your first meditation, try to find the best environment for your mindfulness practice as suggested in the last chapter. A quiet room or corner, a calm atmosphere free of distractions, and a comfortable cushion or chair can facilitate the process.

TIP *Before beginning the first meditation, read the instructions a few times. When you feel that you understand the information, set the instructions aside and begin. If you forget the instructions, don't worry; just let it go. Focus on your breath and continue noticing your experience.*

Basic Mindfulness Meditation (Follow the Breath Meditation)

Here is a basic meditation to help you get started with your practice. It is perfect for beginners, but even advanced practitioners will find it helpful for re-centering and returning to the fundamentals of mindfulness.

Getting Ready

Time

It is important that your mindfulness practice be experienced without stress or pressure. So when you're ready for your first mindfulness meditation, make sure that you can set aside enough time to allow the meditation to be calm and relaxing. Try to plan at least one half hour of undisturbed time, including ten to fifteen minutes for meditating, even if you don't actually meditate for the entire period. Plan to set a clock or timer for the length of time you prefer, so you'll know when you have finished the period of meditation.

Comfort

Before beginning to meditate, take some time to get comfortable. If you're sitting on a cushion, cross your legs loosely in front of you, or leave one leg out straight and bend the other in front without crossing your legs. Be sure that the cushion is high enough to raise your hips above your knees. This relieves pressure and will allow you to remain easily in the pose for a longer time.

If you are sitting on a chair, make sure that your feet are flat on the floor and the base of your back is supported. You may want to place a small cushion or blanket behind you for comfort.

Place your hands, palms down, resting on your thighs in a relaxed manner. If you prefer, an alternative position for your hands is to rest them in your lap, palms up, the left hand gently cupping the right and the tips of the thumbs in easy contact. The position of your hands should allow your arms and shoulders to be relaxed.

Posture

A straight spine is an important component of meditation practice. It allows the breath to flow and the body to relax. To help align your back, imagine a string attached to the top of your head, gently holding up your body so that your spine is erect but the natural curvature is supported. Allow your chin to tilt slightly forward and relax your jaw.

TIP *If, for any reason, you are not able to sit up when meditating, you may do the exercise lying down. Just make sure that you are comfortable and that your breath is not impeded by your position.*

Gaze

If you feel comfortable, close your eyes without squeezing them shut. If you prefer, you can direct your gaze to a spot below you and about four to six feet in front of where you are seated. With your chin slightly tilted, your gaze will naturally go to this spot. Don't try to focus intently, but allow your vision to remain somewhat unclear, even hazy.

Settle In

Feel all your physical sensations as you adjust your body to maximize your comfort. Do you need to alter your position? Is the temperature comfortable or should you modify your clothing? Is your spine supporting you solidly?

Now allow yourself to settle into this easy pose. Experience its stability. Let yourself be connected to your physical self. Inhabit your body.

Follow the Breath Meditation

Begin the breathing meditation by taking three or four deep breaths. Feel the air entering your nostrils, traveling down your throat, filling your lungs, and expanding your abdomen. Now, allow your breath to assume its natural rhythm. Don't try to control it or force it. Don't try to change it or make it "better."

Just be aware that you are breathing. You don't have to make it happen; it just happens. Observe the movement of the breath as it flows into and out of your body. Notice where you feel this movement most distinctly. Perhaps it is most apparent in your nostrils; perhaps you feel it as it causes your abdomen to rise and fall. Wherever you notice the breath, briefly allow your attention to rest there.

Notice the feeling of the breath as your lungs fill with air on inhalation and deflate as you breathe out, the chest expanding and collapsing. Allow your attention to gently travel with the experience of each breath, without evaluation, without comment. Simply watch your breathing. Remain aware of the breath flowing in and flowing out, noticing how it feels.

Now observe the cycle of each breath from the very beginning as it enters the nose or mouth, and follow it as it fills the lungs and expands the chest and the abdomen. Observe the breath as it leaves the body, deflating the abdomen and chest and departing through the nostrils. Remain present for the cycle of each breath, letting your attention gently rest on the awareness of your breath.

Every time you realize that your mind has wandered off the breath—and it will happen often—notice what it was that took you away and then gently bring your attention back to the feeling of the breath coming in and out. No matter how often your mind wanders, simply notice it and bring it back to the breath.

You may find that the mind drifts to thoughts of the past: memories, regrets, accomplishments, or disappointments. Or it may move to anticipation of the future: planning, worrying, wishing, and judging. You may find yourself thinking about what you'll do next after this meditation, what you have to do at work or at home.

When distractions arise—thoughts, images, emotions, sensations—you don't have to *do* anything about them. You don't have to hold on to them or analyze them or judge them. You don't have to decide on that plan; you don't have to replay that conversation; you don't have to reprimand yourself. You just have to breathe. Wherever your thoughts go, just observe them and move on.

Always come back to the breath, to this moment, and allow your breathing to gently cradle you in a state of calm awareness.

Connecting to your breath when distractions are all around is like finding a beautiful shell on the shore. There are many shells, but you are drawn to one and you direct your interest, attention, and movement to that one shell. And though there are many thoughts and feelings floating in your mind, like the multitude of shells on the beach, you direct your awareness to one object: the breath.

Whether your thoughts drift into your mind or clamor for attention, remember that they are just thoughts and have no power and no substance. As you notice them coming, try to distinguish their nature as you let them go. Are they simple thoughts that surface and are easy to release (*I have to get some potatoes for tonight's dinner.*) or are they carrying emotional weight (*I'm really a terrible cook. I don't know why I even bother. Nobody really appreciates what I do anyway.*)?

Whatever the content of your thoughts, whatever emotions they carry, don't try to suppress or ignore them. You can be aware of a thought without elaborating on it, see it without criticizing it, feel it without judging it, and notice it without worrying about it. Just observe the rising thoughts (*This has nothing to do with meditation. I'm not supposed to be bored. What's the matter with me? I'm never going to be really able to meditate.*), accept them, and move your awareness back to the breath. Do this each time the mind wanders.

No matter what kind of thought comes up, you can say to yourself: *That may be a really important issue in my life, but right now is not the time to think about it. Now I'm watching my breath.* Whenever you notice that you have drifted from the present, when you become distracted or restless, you can use the awareness of the breath as a powerful anchor to this moment.

As you focus on your breath, be wholly with the flow of it coming in and going out. For this brief time, allow yourself to *be*, not do.

When the timer sounds, gradually allow yourself to reconnect to the world around you. Your meditation time is done.

TIP *In order to help focus your awareness during the Follow the Breath Meditation, you may want to give yourself a gentle reminder of the breath's rhythm by silently saying "in" as you inhale and "out" as you exhale.*

After You Meditate

After your initial meditation and, in fact, probably after most meditation sessions, you will have some reactions to your experience and possibly a few questions about it.

Writing in your journal after you meditate will help you immediately process the meditation. Looking back at past journal entries will give you access to your experience as it changes over a period of time. You can review days, weeks, or months of your practice and learn about the patterns that your consciousness follows. You may find that sometimes you try too hard or you don't try very much, or that meditation frustrates you, relaxes you, or gives you insights or inspirations. Reading your journal, you may discover that there are particular distractions that are much more common than you realized as well as ones you considered more frequent than they actually are. You may also discover that your meditation practice has been more effective and agreeable than you had remembered. Whatever you learn, it will be a helpful tool as you continue your individual journey of mindfulness practice.

EXERCISE Post-Meditation Journal Entry

End your meditation session with a journal entry. This is a good routine to follow as you continue your mindfulness practice.

JOURNAL PROMPT   *"What did I notice, and how am I feeling about my meditation?"*

Dealing with Challenges

The process of meditating may help us realize many things, but one thing is certain: it teaches us how difficult this simple exercise can actually be. We should expect and prepare to deal with the minor challenges that mindfulness meditation presents. Here are the most

common ones, as well as suggestions for learning from and responding to them.

Physical Discomfort

Although the posture recommended for meditation is intended to be comfortable and promote relaxation, it's not a posture you normally assume for other activities. You may be disconcerted by a feeling that it is awkward or unusual. You may feel strain or pressure from placing your body in a position that is unfamiliar. Sometimes, in the silence and stillness of meditation, you may feel aches and discomfort that you didn't notice in the midst of your usual activity.

Remember, part of the preparation for meditation is inhabiting your body. If all you want to do is get out of it, then the posture you are in is not working for you. If your discomfort is interfering with your ability to focus, then change your position and get comfortable. It's more important to be able to breathe and to focus than to maintain a particular pose. Experiment a little and do what works best for you.

Wandering Thoughts

Having thoughts while meditating is, of course, to be expected and perfectly normal. Mindfulness meditation is not intended as a way to get rid of our thoughts, which are themselves the raw materials for our mindfulness practice. However, mindfulness training helps us deal with those thoughts in a healthful fashion.

With mindfulness, we begin to develop a different relationship with our thoughts. We begin to see them as just thoughts, not facts. They are not reality, but merely our interpretation of it. When we are more aware of our thoughts and can see them clearly, we are freer to make choices about whether and how to act.

When we meditate, not only do our thoughts roam, but they can wander in directions that are painful, unpleasant, embarrassing, or distressing. These thoughts don't have any effect on the value of our meditation exercise. They simply provide an opportunity to let them be, to let yourself be. The work of meditation is to see those thoughts and to accept them, without judgment, without comment.

Despite this advice about the value of wandering thoughts, you're probably going to find yourself criticizing them anyway. That's natural, too. Just observe the process of condemnation as another distraction, and then return to the breath.

When you notice that you are distracted by wandering thoughts, gently bring your attention back to the object of your meditation. This is how you begin to relate differently to distractions and increase your ability to focus and concentrate.

Forgetting the Exercise

If we are doing a meditation from memory, it's natural to forget parts of it. We may leave out some elements and even include some elements that were not in the instructions. With mindfulness meditation, this is no problem. The essential elements of every meditation are very clear and very simple: Bring your awareness to the present and accept what you notice without judgment. So when your meditation is a focus on the awareness of breath, the only important things are continuing to bring your attention back to the breath and noticing your experience with nonjudgmental acceptance. If you forget something, just notice that, too.

Time Limits

Although it is ideal to have sufficient time to meditate for at least ten to fifteen minutes each session, sometimes that is not possible. Mindfulness meditation doesn't require any set time or any set procedure; it is accommodating. Just keep in mind that you always have everything essential with you—your body, breath, and mind. So whether you have two minutes or twenty minutes, devoting the time you do have to an awareness of your breath helps cultivate mindfulness and develop your practice.

Distractions

You can try to ensure a time for meditation that is free of distractions by, for example, selecting a space that is away from the traffic flow in the household, choosing a time when other household members are normally away or occupied, and switching off all phones and electronic devices. But whatever plans you make and however many precautions you take, it is likely that some distractions will occur that interfere with your meditation. If it's not a crisis to which you have to respond, you can try incorporating the distraction into your meditation. Notice any sounds, and accept them nonjudgmentally. If that doesn't work, you can end the meditation and return to it later in the day. Remember, mindfulness is not about eliminating distractions; it's about learning to deal with them with equanimity.

"Monkey Mind"

If we approach mindfulness meditation with the goal of stopping our thoughts, we are fighting an uphill battle. And, in fact, our thoughts are a rich and rewarding part of being human. In mindfulness meditation, we don't want to stop thinking; we want to learn to distinguish between thinking and being lost in our thoughts. Often we may try to be in the present, yet our mind hops around or tries to take us on long, winding journeys. We want to learn how to focus the monkey mind.

Sometimes such thoughts seem compelling, sometimes nonsensical, sometimes repellant. Mindfulness meditation can help us understand that thoughts are not who we are; they are just thoughts. And whatever thoughts we have, they contribute to our meditation. When we find our mind leaping from thought to thought and chattering away, we should just notice it, accept it, and bring our focus back to our breath. We should not think of wandering thoughts as a problem, but rather as fodder for our meditation. We can use them for observation, reflection, understanding, learning, and deepening our practice.

Restlessness and Drowsiness

Both normal experiences during meditation, restlessness and drowsiness are the flip side of each other and an indication that, at that moment, we are not experiencing tranquility. We can approach these two states with an open mind and not add weight to them with judgments: *I shouldn't be feeling this . . . I'm terrible at meditating.* And we can observe them with curiosity and not struggle with them: *What parts of my body want to move? Do I have to move now? Where am I feeling the fatigue? Can I list all the places that feel tired?*

To gently compensate for drowsiness, we can change position, open our eyes, or stand for a moment. If feeling restless, we can change the focus of our meditation, for example, by shifting from our breath to the sounds in the room.

Erratic Practice

Sometimes it seems like we just have no time; sometimes it seems like our practice isn't getting anywhere; sometimes it just seems boring, frustrating, or annoying to try to keep a commitment to mindfulness. When having such thoughts, it is helpful to remember that the most effective way to build a mindfulness muscle is to practice.

Practice doesn't have to mean meditating each day for one hour or even necessarily ten minutes. But it does mean a regular and serious commitment to mindfulness. This may take the form of daily meditation. It may take the form of taking mindful breaths when you wake up and before going to sleep. It may mean that each day you assume your meditative posture for five minutes during your lunch break and focus on the sounds in your workplace. It may involve mindful eating one meal each day. Whatever you decide, it's important to try to integrate some mindfulness practice into your daily life. Before you know it, mindfulness will be part of your regular routine.

Regular Practice

Try having meditation practice for a few minutes each day, whether you feel like doing it or not. Training the mind simply to follow the very natural process of breathing—letting yourself merge with the sensation of breath—helps tame the monkey mind that swings out of control from one thought to the next. Simply be aware of how it feels to spend some time each day just being with your breath without having to *do* anything.

TIP *Schedule time for your mindfulness practice just as you would for an appointment. Experiment with different times to discover what works best for you.*

If you meditate on your breath regularly, over time you will find yourself returning to the breath throughout the day, even when you're not meditating. When you feel stress, anger, jealousy, sadness, or pain, you'll be able to acknowledge it and come back to your breathing. Mindfulness will not only become a practice—it will be woven into how you lead your life. In working to experience life directly, just by "sitting and doing nothing" during mindfulness meditation, you will be doing an incredible amount for your well-being.

———————————————

Let us not look back in anger, nor forward in fear,
but around in awareness.

—James Thurber, *Credos and Curios*

CHAPTER FIVE

Simple Meditations for Common Concerns

As has been reiterated, mindfulness meditation is not goal oriented. We cannot expect mindfulness to eliminate stress or stop pain or put us to sleep. But we *can* expect it to help us develop a different relationship with the issues in our lives that vex us, frustrate us, worry us, or give us pain. And, paradoxically, when we don't ignore things, but instead we attend to them—and when we don't try to change things, but instead we accept them—we often discover that altering our relationship has altered how we experience a particular issue. The pain may still be present, but we suffer less. The stress is still there, but we are less distressed by it.

So mindfulness meditation has no specific goals except awareness and acceptance. But some meditations, although not intended to fix the issues that are problems for us, do help us focus on them in a way that can change our relationship with them. In this chapter, you'll find five meditations cued to common issues of modern daily life, including stress, lack of focus, anxiety, negative thought patterns, and insomnia.

TIP *Before doing other mindfulness meditation practices, it is a good idea to feel comfortable with the Follow the Breath Meditation (page 50). This is a powerful tool that becomes part of every other mindfulness meditation and helps us focus.*

Stress

The stress response results when a perceived threat triggers a primitive fight-or-flight reaction. It involves many body systems: the blood flow goes to our extremities, preparing us for action; the heart beats faster; the breathing becomes more rapid; the glands release stress hormones—we are prepared for action.

But when our body is ready for action and we don't actually fight or run, we don't give our body the chance to come out of the state of hyperarousal. When this happens frequently—when we are always afraid of being late for work, or we're worried that our kids will hang out with a dangerous crowd, or we think that we'll never find a partner to love us—we end up in a state of chronic stress. Not only does our body respond to the perceived threats, but the responses—rapid breathing and heartbeat, sweaty palms—that our body has even to distressing thoughts communicate to our minds that we are under attack, even when nothing is happening at that moment. Essentially, our body overreacts to something and then convinces us that we have something to react to.

The mindfulness meditation known as the Body Scan Meditation helps us be aware of what is actually going on in our body. It puts us in contact with our physiological experience as it is happening, in the moment.

Body Scan Meditation

Getting Ready

Schedule at least one half hour to do this exercise. Minimize distractions; turn off phones and other devices. Sit on a cushion with your legs loosely crossed or in a comfortable chair that supports your back with your feet flat on the floor. Some people prefer to do this exercise lying down with legs and arms outstretched, although this increases the likelihood of falling asleep during the meditation.

Getting Grounded

Before you begin, notice the parts of your body in contact with the chair, floor, cushion, or mat. If you feel any particular pressure at the points of contact, imagine that your body is softening there and you can allow it to be supported. Close your eyes if it feels comfortable, or cast your gaze low. Take a few deep breaths and then allow yourself to breathe naturally, inhaling and exhaling in your own rhythm. Let everything but your body fade into the background.

TIP *If you are lying down and you notice yourself falling asleep, do the meditation with your eyes open.*

Scanning

Imagine that you are taking a tour of your body, starting with your feet. You will not be altering or moving your body parts; you'll simply be noticing them as they are at that moment. As you bring your awareness to each part of your body, imagine your breath traveling with your attention, flowing to that part of the body as you observe it. If at any time while you are scanning your body your mind wanders—as it certainly will—just notice what your thoughts are and bring your attention back to your breath and the part of the body on which you are focusing. Once you scan over a body part, allow that part to fade from awareness. Let it go and then move up to the next body part.

TIP *While scanning, if you encounter a sensation that is unpleasant, you may try to push it away, or feel angry or fearful. See if you can let go of that reaction and experience the sensation directly, without interpretation or judgment.*

To begin the Body Scan Meditation, move your attention to focus on your feet. You may notice the ground under your feet, or some tingling, or the feel of your shoes or clothing in contact with your feet. You may feel pressure or tightness or space. Feel the temperature of each of the parts of your feet. Notice your toes, heels, the arches, the tops and sides of your feet. Allow yourself to observe all your sensations. Avoid judging or criticizing your experience. Just notice.

Now move your attention to your ankles, shins, and calves. Notice any sensations that might be present there. If there is any tightness in your muscles, try to let go of that resistance and tightness, and simply notice the sensations. You may notice the feel of your clothing, or the air, or even an ache. Just allow yourself to be aware of it as a sensation in your body.

Move on, bringing your attention to your knees and the backs of your knees. Pay attention to any sensations in this part of your body. What do you notice? Any aches or discomfort? Avoid judging; just observe your knees and the sensations in that area with acceptance.

Shift your attention to your thighs. Experience the difference between the backs and fronts of your thighs. Feel the contact of your clothing, the pressure of the chair or floor. Be aware of the temperature on your skin. Simply notice your thighs. If you find tightness or tension in this area, try letting it go as you observe. When your mind wanders, remember to just notice what it is doing. Then come back to focusing on your breath and the part of the body you are observing.

Move your focus to the "sit bones," buttocks, and pelvic area. Once again, you may notice sensations like tension, temperature, or the feel of clothing as you observe this area. Remember, as you notice sensations, to avoid criticizing, judging, appreciating, or disliking them. If your mind is judging, ruminating, or wandering, simply bring your attention back to your breath and continue to observe this area of your body.

Continue observing your body, moving your attention to the abdomen and lower back, scanning those areas for sensations. Can you feel the rise and fall of your abdomen as you breathe? Is the small of your back in contact with support? Allow your abdomen to soften and your back to relax as you experience your sensations. Breathe naturally as you observe the rhythm of your breath.

Allow your awareness to include your upper abdomen and middle back. What do you notice here? Do you feel any tightness or tension? Do not resist any sensations; just observe them. Notice the life in your body as it communicates to you what is going on through these sensations. Allow yourself to be with the sensations, making sure your breath is flowing naturally and comfortably.

Expand your attention to your chest and upper back. Notice whatever sensations are there. Allow them just to be present. Do not judge, evaluate, or reject them. When your mind wanders, notice it. Allow the thoughts to pass by, gently moving your attention back to your breath and the body part you are observing.

Shift your awareness to your shoulders. Notice the sensations there, whatever they might be. If you're holding tension in your shoulders, let it go. Allow your shoulders to relax and continue to scan them, noticing anything that comes up.

Move your attention to your arms. Begin scanning from your shoulders down to your elbows and then down to your wrists, hands, and fingers. Notice any sensations present for you. You may be aware of your arms touching other parts of your body, or your clothing, or the air around them. You may notice your muscles; if you find tension there, simply let go of it and continue to observe these areas of your body.

Now observe your neck. Observe your throat and back of your neck. Be aware of the sides of your neck, noticing whatever is there. Is there tightness, tingling, hair touching your skin? Whatever is there, just notice it. Avoid judging, liking, or criticizing what you notice. Simply be aware of this part of your body, and see if you can let go of any tension you might observe. Breathe and relax with your breath as you focus on this part of your body.

Shift your attention next to your head—the back, sides, and top. Simply notice whatever sensations you perceive there. Observe your forehead, your temples, your jaw. If you experience any tension or tightness, simply let it go. If there is any pain or discomfort, notice it as a sensation. Some sensations in this area might be very subtle, so it is necessary to really focus your awareness.

Continue to scan down your face, eyes, cheekbones, ears, hair, chin. Pay attention to the sensations you notice. Whatever is there, just notice it, kindly observing without judgment, breathing naturally.

Finally, connect your whole body together. Feel your head connected to your neck, your neck connected to your torso, your torso connected to your arms and legs, your limbs connected to your hands and feet. Feel the skin around your whole body. Observe the wholeness of your body.

Gradually open your eyes and bring the meditation to a close.

Lack of Focus

The ability to multitask is often promoted as a necessary skill in the modern age. But what's really happening is that we focus on numerous activities at once and do not actually give our full attention to any *one* thing. Many of us keep a list of all the tasks that still need to be finished. And those never-completed lists lead us to feel frustrated, guilty, and dissatisfied.

Mindfulness brings concentration. Just by focusing on one task at a time and giving it all your attention, you are increasing your ability to concentrate. When you drink water mindfully, for example, you are concentrating on drinking. If you are concentrating, you can experience life more fully and experience greater satisfaction. You feel more stable, more connected, and better able to attend to your tasks. When you drive mindfully, you are safer; when you speak mindfully, you are better able to say what you mean; when you eat mindfully, you improve your control, your digestion, and your appreciation.

When you learn to concentrate on the task at hand, you are disciplining your mind. Practicing mindfulness in any one way helps us incorporate mindfulness in all ways. One of the many useful ways to exercise our capacity to focus is to practice mindful eating.

TIP   *Remember that mindfulness involves a suspension of judgment for a reason: it's hard to do! So when you notice your mind wandering away from the task at hand, simply note that this has happened and return your attention back to your intended focus. Repeat as many times as necessary. There is no way to fail.*

Mindful eating may seem like a simple task. You decide what you want to eat, prepare it, and then eat it. But if you take the time to be fully aware of your changing states of attention while you eat food, you might be surprised at how little of your consciousness is typically present as you eat. You might be watching TV, making a shopping list, replaying an argument, surfing the Internet, or planning your evening. You may be eating, but your mind is often somewhere else.

The Orange Meditation can help you focus on the actual experience of eating. It can make you aware of what you are eating and how you are eating it now, in the present. Buddhist teacher and practitioner Thích Nhất Hạnh recommends the Orange Meditation not only to improve concentration, but as a life-altering practice:

"When we are mindful, we recognize what we are picking up. When we put it into our mouth, we know what we are putting into our mouth. When we chew it, we know what we are chewing. It's very simple. When you are truly here, contemplating the orange, breathing and smiling, the orange becomes a miracle. It is enough to bring you a lot of happiness. You peel the orange, smell it, take a section, and put

*it in your mouth mindfully, fully aware of the juice on your
tongue. This is eating an orange in mindfulness. It makes
the miracle of life possible. It makes joy possible."*

Orange Meditation

Getting Ready

Schedule at least ten minutes to do this exercise. Sit in a comfortable chair. Select an orange for your practice, and place it on a table in front of you or hold it in the palm of your hand.

Getting Grounded

Close your eyes for a moment and take a few deep breaths. Then allow yourself to breathe naturally, inhaling and exhaling in your own rhythm. Lift the orange in the palm of your hand so that you can examine it thoroughly. Let everything else but the orange fade into the background.

TIP *This meditation doesn't have to be about an orange. You can select any fruit or vegetable you want to eat—a peach, an apple, a tomato, a lettuce leaf. Just substitute your selection for the orange in the instructions.*

Seeing the Orange

Look at the orange as you breathe in and out. Allow yourself to really see the orange. Identify it in your mind: *This is an orange.* Notice the appearance of the orange. Is the color vibrant? Is it deeply textured or almost smooth? Is it large or small? Is the skin thick or thin? Notice all the visual characteristics of the orange.

Examining the Orange

Slowly begin the process of peeling the orange. Notice the amount of effort it takes. Observe the flesh of the fruit as the skin is peeled back. Take in the orange scent as you reveal the fruit's interior. Notice the contrasting colors inside the fruit. Is the flesh pale or vibrant? Is the smell fresh or dull?

If your mind begins to wander (*I must remember to get the oil in my car changed.*) or judge (*This is taking too long . . . I just want to eat it.*), bring it back to the breath and awareness of the orange. Do this as often as you find your mind moving away from your focus.

Eating the Orange

Take a section of the orange and put it in your mouth mindfully. Allow yourself to be fully aware of the juice on your tongue. Take one bite. As you do, notice the different textures. Is the slice fresh? Is it juicy? Is it chewy?

Do not swallow right away. Notice any changes in the textures or flavor as you continue to chew. Savor each bite as long as possible. When you have swallowed the first bite, pause before you take the next bite. Notice how your mouth feels when it is empty. Repeat this process each time you take a bite. Bring all your attention to what you are doing. If your mind wanders—perhaps to a memory of eating an orange at another time, perhaps to something that has nothing to do with your present focus—bring it back to eating the orange. Simply notice the food itself and the sensations of eating.

Focus on the sensations you feel in your mouth and digestive tract as well as in other areas of your body: the movement of your hands and arms as you bring the food to your mouth, the feel of your body in contact with the chair, the sounds you hear as you eat, the sounds you may make as you eat, the aroma of the orange. Eat slowly and notice everything.

When you have finished eating the orange, sit for a few moments breathing naturally, appreciating the orange you just ate.

Anxiety

When we are anxious, we usually get hijacked by our thoughts; we think about everything that could go wrong and imagine worst-case scenarios about the future. When we do this, we generally can't notice the pleasant experiences all around us. In fact, we rarely notice *any* experiences.

It can be very difficult to sit and meditate with an agitated mind. We may try to focus, but every attempt is deflected by worry: *My boss will think I'm wasting time if she finds out I'm meditating. I don't really have time for this—I'd better get up. I'll never be able to finish that project.* We try to convince ourselves not to go down that path, but even our efforts to stop worrying may end up with judgments and self-criticisms.

If we are beset by anxiety, much of the time we are caught up in our mental world—ruminating about the past, imagining the future, planning, worrying, evaluating. A mindfulness exercise called Walking Meditation can help short-circuit some of this process and replace preoccupation with a focus that engages our mind with a physical activity. We can use walking mindfulness briefly throughout the day—as we walk to the car or to a friend's house, for example—or we can use it as a specific part of our meditation practice.

Walking Meditation

With the Walking Meditation, we bring our attention to the physical act of walking. We bring mindfulness to an activity we normally do without much conscious thought. In the Walking Meditation, we deliberately focus on what is often a mechanical act and we become aware, step by step, of how our body moves from place to place. We center our consciousness in the feet, not the head.

Getting Ready

When you plan on doing this exercise as a meditation rather than as a mindfulness activity in everyday life, try to set aside at least fifteen or twenty minutes to complete it. It is best not to combine it with anything else, such as physical exercise or shopping, so that you will be able to concentrate on the meditation without adding distractions. It's beneficial to do the exercise outdoors if possible—perhaps in a park, for example, where you have space to move freely. Otherwise, try to find an area indoors that will permit you to take at least twenty steps without having to turn.

Getting Grounded

Before you begin to walk, spend a little time standing still. Get into a comfortable position, feet shoulder-width apart, weight evenly distributed, arms either down by your sides or hands clasped lightly behind you. Become aware of your body. Take a few deep breaths and then allow your breathing to return to its normal rhythm.

Bring your attention to your feet. Feel all the parts of your feet—the toes, arches, soles, tops, sides, and heels. Feel the sensation of your feet inside your shoes (if you have them on) and feel your feet making contact with the ground or floor. Experience the sensations as your feet touch the ground: Does it feel hard or giving, rough or smooth, stable or shifting? Do your feet feel weighted to the ground or in light contact? Allow yourself to simply feel all the sensations as your feet are touching the ground. Let go of judgments. Don't evaluate. Just observe.

Now shift your weight to the left foot. Give your attention to the changes you feel—any balance shifting, muscles tensing, skin stretching. Slowly shift back, re-centering your weight and noticing how your body feels now. Then shift your weight to the right and observe these sensations. Don't compare, don't analyze, just observe. Stand comfortably for a moment, breathing naturally.

Walking

Begin walking at a relaxed, fairly slow, but normal pace. Put your attention on the physical act of walking, giving your awareness to the movement in your legs and feet. You will be conscious of the sights and sounds around you, but maintain your focus on your feet as they touch the ground, step by step. It is natural to find your attention drawn to the external environment as you walk, but keep bringing your attention to what is going on with your body.

Notice how the soles of your feet feel—the contact they make with your socks or shoes, the textures of the fabrics touching them, the way they feel as they bear the weight of your body, and the sensations in them as you walk along. Feel how each of your feet moves, touching the ground with each step.

Now slow your pace a little. As you walk, separate the placement of each foot into a series of movements. Lift the heel, and then lift the sole. Move the foot forward through the air, and place the foot on the ground. Finish one step completely before you begin the next. Pay attention to the movement, bringing your awareness to every sensation as you walk slowly and with mindfulness.

TIP *Until you become familiar with the Walking Meditation, you may feel a little shaky and unbalanced. If that happens, move a little more quickly until you feel steadier. Then slow down again as you continue.*

Occasionally, allow your awareness to move from your feet up your entire body, noticing the sensations as you walk: the swinging of your arms and hips, the alternating movement of your legs, the position of your head as you stride. Give your attention sequentially to all the parts of your body: ankles, shins, calves, knees, thighs, hips, pelvis, back, chest, shoulders, arms, neck, and head. As you become aware of each part, notice the sensations in that part of your body—any stiffness or tension, ease or softness.

If you feel tension anywhere, let it go. Let the meditation be like a slow dance, thoughtful and enjoyable. When your mind wanders, bring it back to your feet and the movement as you walk—one foot at a time, step by step.

When you have been walking for fifteen or twenty minutes, just stop and stand still. Allow yourself to feel your sensations at that moment, in that place. Notice how your body feels standing still. Notice how your feet feel, in contact with the ground, supported by it. Take a few deep breaths and gently close the meditation.

Negative Thought Patterns

While it is common to have occasional negative thoughts, excessive negative thought patterns can fill life with recriminations, regrets, and unhappiness and can contribute to anxiety, stress, anger, and depression. Physical consequences can include digestion disorders and a weakened immune system.

Negative thoughts often revolve around what's wrong—with our friends, with our work, with our family, with our life. Our attention may become fixated on and exaggerate the negative, while often minimizing what is going well. We may try to halt negative thinking with a variety of tactics. Distraction, diversions, and planning to think positively can hold an initial appeal, but these temporary efforts can often end with a return to the same defeating thought patterns.

Working with our emotions in meditation, however, can sharpen our ability to recognize negative thoughts as soon as they begin and free us to deal with them rather than react to them—we don't have to try to ignore them and we don't have to allow them to control us.

Emotions Meditation

Getting Ready

Schedule at least one half hour to do this exercise. Minimize distractions, such as phones or TVs. Sit on a cushion with your legs loosely crossed or in a comfortable chair that supports your back, with your feet flat on the floor. Place your hands palms down on your thighs, or your left hand cupping the right, palms up.

Getting Grounded

Before you start the meditation, do a brief scan of your physical sensations. Notice the parts of your body in contact with the chair or the floor, cushion, or mat. If you feel any particular pressure at the points of contact, imagine that your body is softening there and you can allow it to be supported. Close your eyes if it feels comfortable, or cast your gaze low. Take a few deep breaths and then allow yourself to breathe naturally, inhaling and exhaling in your own rhythm. Notice the emotions you are experiencing as you prepare to meditate. Do you feel happy, anxious, calm, bored? Just take a brief note of your general emotional experience at that moment.

TIP *In order to stay present when you become aware that a thought or feeling is carrying you away from your focus, try the technique of mental noting. This means using a simple one-word label—a "note"—to name what you are experiencing right at that moment. Noting can interrupt the persistent flow of thoughts.*

Mental noting does not involve analysis or judgment. It is a simple naming of the current experience. For example, upon hearing a sound, you can note "hearing," or upon noticing a thought, note "thinking." You can note emotions ("sad"), sensations ("cold"), and even mental activity ("remembering").

Silently repeat your noting word two or three times.

Observing and Accepting Emotions

Begin the meditation by focusing on your breath, noticing as it comes in and goes out. Continue following your breath, noting any emotions as they rise up and move into your awareness. Continue focusing on your breath. As you observe your breath and notice your emotions, be aware if any particular emotion seems to recur or be especially powerful. Make that emotion the focus of this meditation.

See if you can locate that emotion in your body. Are you feeling it in your stomach, your shoulder, or your throat? What are the physical sensations you experience with that emotion? Are you queasy? Are your hands clenched? Do you have butterflies? Is your heart racing?

Continue to be aware of the emotion and the sensations in your body. Allow yourself to remain with the experience, as though you are witnessing it. Try not to judge or evaluate it. Just be aware of it, in a gentle and relaxed way. It is common to want to resist, change, or ignore difficult emotions, but here you are accepting them as part of your experience, fully, without the need to push them away.

If you are aware of the emotion residing in one part of your body, try to relax it. For example, if you notice that your fists are clenched, open them slowly. If your shoulders are hunched, lower them gently. If your stomach is tight, use your breath to soften it.

As you release the tension in one part of your body, you may notice tension in another part as well. Relax and release the tension, part by part, wherever you notice it. Continue observing the emotion. You may find that noticing the emotion with your body in a more relaxed state helps you observe the emotion itself more calmly. You can let go of struggling with it and just see it as it is—just an emotion.

You are not using the meditation to suppress your feelings and emotions, but to free them. You can become more familiar with how they arise and what they actually feel like when you do not react to them or repress them. You can perceive your experience in a way that gives you access to your emotions in a different way. You can simply let them be.

If you find the emotion overwhelming, return to the focus on your breath. If you feel paralyzed by negative emotions like fear or despair, open your eyes to bring you back to the present. You can do this at any point during the meditation. If you find yourself judging or criticizing your emotion, return to the awareness of the present experience. Focus on what is happening right then in your body, the emotion you are feeling right at that moment.

Finally, return to the focus on your breath, bringing your awareness back to the rise and fall of your chest and abdomen as you inhale and exhale. Slowly open your eyes and bring the meditation to an end.

Insomnia

Some people may take a good night's sleep for granted, but for the majority of Americans, that restorative state is often elusive. You want to turn off all the mental chatter so you can rest. However, your mind does not always cooperate. You may close your eyes but still see images of the past day and visions of the day to come. Mindfulness has proven to be a powerful tool in reducing or eliminating this hyper-aroused state. It can help restore the balance within and allow you to rest.

The following exercise, the Mindfulness at Night Meditation, is not designed to make you go to sleep, but rather to increase your awareness and understanding of your mind at night. It may or may not result in sleep, but it will help you let go of the day.

Mindfulness at Night Meditation

Getting Ready

If you have any evening routines, finish them all before you get into bed. Turn off all electronic devices, and turn off or dim the lights. Once you are lying comfortably in bed, take five deep breaths, breathing in through the nose and out through the mouth. As you breathe in, try to get a sense of your lungs filling with air and your chest expanding. As you breathe out, imagine any feelings of tension in your body just melting away.

Getting Grounded

Allow yourself to notice how you are feeling both mentally and physically. Take your time with this. There's no need to rush. It is likely that you will notice many thoughts cascading through your mind (this is normal). Just let them be there. Avoid the temptation to resist the thoughts, no matter how unsettling or uncomfortable they may be. Don't fight with them, just note them.

Next, become aware of physical sensations. Bring your attention to the sensation of your body touching the bed, the weight of your body sinking down into the mattress. Notice where the points of contact are strongest. Is the weight distributed evenly? Are there any places where you feel discomfort? You can make minor adjustments to increase your comfort level and then return to focusing on the breath for a few more moments. You may also notice sounds that are present. Don't resist any sounds, even if you are tempted to keep your focus on them. Gently rest your awareness on a sound briefly, and then bring your attention back to your breath.

Scanning Your Body

Now focus on getting a sense of how your body feels. Mentally scan your body from your toes to the top of your head. Observe any tension or tightness, and also be aware of any areas that feel soft and relaxed. You can do this scan several times, noting any changes as you repeat the process. Do not linger on any particular parts of the body, even if your mind wants to stay with areas of tension. Just note the sensations you feel and move on.

Bring your attention to the part of your body where you are experiencing the breath most clearly. It might be your nostrils or throat, chest or abdomen. Just note where you feel the breath and continue breathing naturally. Notice the characteristics of the breath. Is it long or short, deep or shallow? Just notice without evaluating. There is no required way to breathe for this meditation.

Your mind will naturally wander while you are attending to your breathing. Each time you notice this, bring your awareness again to the breath, noting each time as you inhale and exhale. When you are ready, you can begin the next part of the meditation.

Quick Replay

Now you will review your day in a focused and structured way. Begin with the first moment you can remember in the day, right after waking up. Then using a relaxed "fast-forward," allow yourself to watch as your mind replays the events and conversations of the day. This should not be in detail; try to just see yourself going through the day almost as though you are on a moving sidewalk, seeing the day pass by, but not stopping at any point.

This replay of your day should take only a few minutes. You will probably experience the temptation to linger at different points and get caught up in mulling over what you are seeing. You may want to replay a conversation or redo an event, or just stay stuck in a powerful feeling. Remember you are moving on and cannot linger. You can only observe and keep going. If you get distracted, note the distraction, bring your attention back to the breath, pick up where you left off, and continue. Bring yourself up to the present moment.

Turning Off the Body

Having arrived at the present moment, allow yourself to be fully here now. Return your focus to your body. Beginning with the small toe of your left foot, imagine that you are turning it off for the night, putting it to rest. Do the same with the next toe and the next, the sole of the foot, the arch, the ball of the foot, the top, the heel. Move on to your ankle, shin, knee, and so on, up to your left hip and pelvic area. Do this slowly and deliberately, focusing your awareness directly on each part of your body as you turn it off. Before you begin this process with the right foot and leg, pause briefly to notice any variation between the left leg and the right. Be aware of any differences in tightness and tension, relaxation and ease.

Repeat the process, turning off your right foot, leg, and pelvic area. Continue the exercise through the torso, down each arm to the hand and fingers. Take the time to really turn off each body part, almost allowing it to float away as you disengage it. Gradually move up through your throat, neck, face, and head. Now notice the sensation of your whole body having been turned off—the muscles, joints, and all the body parts freed from work and allowed to rest and relax.

You can now just stay focused on this relaxed awareness of your body. Perhaps you'll drift off to sleep; you may even fall asleep before completing the exercise. Or perhaps you are not asleep. Whatever your experience, don't judge or criticize it or worry about the results. Remember that the meditation is not an exercise to make you fall asleep, but rather a meditation to increase your awareness of, and attention to, your mind at night.

Now that you have learned some meditations to help you better deal with specific areas of concern, let's move on to the next step: bringing mindfulness into your life not just through meditation, but on the spot in everyday situations.

How we spend our days is, of course,
how we spend our lives. What we do with this hour, and
that one, is what we are doing.

—Annie Dillard, _The Writing Life_

CHAPTER SIX

Mindfulness in Everyday Life

The key to mindfulness is practice. And the key to practicing mindfulness is just to focus your attention on this moment, as it is happening, and to do it often. In addition to regular meditation practice, you can cultivate mindfulness more informally by placing your awareness on your moment-to-moment experience during everyday activities.

The actions that we perform on a daily basis often become the most mindless because we habitually cruise through them on autopilot. But these activities serve as wonderful opportunities to practice mindfulness. Do one thing at a time and give it your full attention. As you pet the cat, eat an apple, or walk to the car, slow down the process and be fully present. Allow it to unfold and involve all your senses, all your being.

TIP *Remember that mindfulness is about connecting with life and experiencing it more fully. So while it is important to make a commitment to bringing mindfulness into your life, it is equally important to be flexible about your efforts. Rather than judging your actions, just learn from what you do or don't do.*

Daily Mindfulness Practices

You can practice mindfulness throughout the day, every day:

- **Waking up.** Before you get out of bed, pause and notice your breathing. Focus on how you feel at that moment.

- **Showering.** Pay attention to all your sensations as you shower—the temperature and pressure of the water on your skin, the scent of the soap, the sound of water as it flows, the feel of your bare feet on the tiles. Really bring yourself into the moment and actually think about what you are doing. Notice how this mindful experience may differ from your usual routine.

- **Eating breakfast.** Notice what you are eating and be aware of your sensations as you eat. Pay attention as you bite, as you chew, as you swallow. Notice the smells, flavors, and textures of your food. Note your emotions as you begin the day. Are you nervous, excited, happy, sad? Pause and take a few relaxing breaths when you have finished eating.

- **Walking.** Walk mindfully, aware of how your feet touch the floor or ground and how your body moves through space. Slow your pace and think about the movement rather than the destination.

- **Standing.** Take a mindful pause if you are waiting for a train or bus. Be conscious of your surroundings—the smells, the sounds, the other people. Allow your attention to rest lightly on all the elements of your environment.

- **Driving.** If you are driving, take a mindful moment when you are stopped at a red light. Notice your hands on the steering wheel, any tension in your shoulders. Take a breath and relax.

- **Getting to work.** Start your workday with a brief mindful moment. Breathe deeply a few times and experience the sensations in your body.

- **Pausing mindfully.** At any moment during the day you can take a mindful pause. It's important to sometimes stop doing and simply be. Observe your breath, observe your body. If only briefly, create an island of peace in the sea of distractions.

- **Eating lunch.** Occasionally, perhaps once a week or more, select a quiet place to eat alone. Use this time to eat mindfully. Pay attention to all your senses and eat slowly. Think about where your food came from—the fields where it grew, the sun that nourished it, the workers who farmed or prepared it. Look, smell, feel. Examine your food. Take a bite, chew, taste, and swallow. Enjoy.

- **Preparing to go home.** Take a moment to reflect briefly on your day. Did it go well? What might you have changed? Just note the events, don't linger on them or judge them. Breathe and let them go.

- **Arriving home.** Take a moment to take a breath, notice your surroundings, and experience your body in this place. Be present.

Mindful Listening

At home, work, school, or wherever you are, you can also practice mindful listening. This means you just listen without judgment and without preparing or thinking about your response or opinion. You allow the other person to express their ideas and feelings without interruption, without adding your opinion, without expressing immediate agreement or disagreement. Just listen.

Although practicing mindful listening may not always work in a business meeting or class where you are expected to provide a quick reaction or opinion, at other times, listening mindfully may provide you with information and insights about your employer and colleagues that can improve your work effectiveness. In relationships, mindful listening can promote mutual respect and help create a deep bond of understanding.

Keeping Your Mindfulness Journal

A mindfulness journal can become an important part of your everyday practice. Mindfulness is about knowing where you are at the moment. It is an awareness of where you have been, through reflection on your experiences. It is also about making choices about where you want to go, supported by the clarity your mindfulness practice provides. Writing in a mindfulness journal can enhance all of these areas of awareness, helping connect the past, present, and future, so that life seems more of an integrated whole, rather than a collection of separate experiences.

TIP *When you keep a mindfulness journal, sometimes an anticipation of what you are planning to write can come up during meditation and interfere with your focus on the present. Just acknowledge such thoughts and let go of them, without self-criticism, and then return to the practice.*

Keeping a mindfulness journal helps clarify what is actually going on with your practice. Taking a few minutes to write about your experiences while meditating can help you discern some areas to work on developing. For example, do you notice that you are often weighed down by negative thinking? Do you need greater focus on your breathing? Are you only meditating when you're tired? Whatever you discover, you can adjust your practice to address it.

A mindfulness journal also allows you to reflect on your experience as it has changed over time. You can review several days, weeks, or months of your practice and learn about the patterns that your consciousness follows. You may discover, for instance, that there are particular distractions that commonly arise or objects of focus that are most effective.

Keeping a mindfulness journal can help you set goals for your meditation practice. Looking back at your past experience lets you see what you may want to work on. Perhaps you notice that acceptance, patience, or calmness is difficult for you. Maybe it's committing to more regular practice or connecting to your physical sensations. You can use whatever comes up frequently in the journal to guide the focus of your practice.

A mindfulness journal can be used to help draw your awareness to a particular element of a meditation session. You may, for example, write down all the judgments you make during one meditation session—probably many more than you would have expected. You can then reflect on any patterns you see. Do you mainly judge yourself or others? Are your judgments about activities or characteristics? What emotions are connected to your judgments? Are you frequently judging the meditation practice itself? All of this information can help you see these judgments as just thoughts and let them go.

When you write in your journal, note the date, the name of the meditation practice you used that day, and how long you meditated. Then you can write any comments on your practice experience: what distractions you had, what you used to try to refocus, what you felt (calmness, concentration, annoyance, etc.). You might write about any factors in your life that had an effect on your practice—things like lack of sleep, a particularly busy day, or the completion of a project.

In addition to writing about your meditation sessions, you can use your journal to identify how mindfulness has had an impact on your everyday life—for example, how your relationship with food might have changed, any difference in your sense of calmness, any shift in your perspective on concerns and your approach to problem solving. Some of these changes may seem significant (*My sleep is a lot better.*), while others may seem less important (*I never realized how much I liked asparagus.*). Any shift in perspective is important to note as part of your mindfulness practice.

Another way of making your journal valuable is by using it to explore some ideas mindfully. You can use prompts to increase your awareness of your thoughts and emotions in the moment. Here are some prompts to get you started.

- *What I am feeling in this moment is . . .*
- *Today I hope to . . .*
- *What is really bothering me now is . . .*
- *My strengths are . . .*
- *I would never be able to . . .*
- *I love . . .*
- *I would like to thank . . .*
- *My body feels . . .*
- *I am really interested in . . .*
- *People always . . .*
- *I'd like to improve my relationship with . . .*
- *What stops me is . . .*
- *I've been lying to myself about . . .*
- *I remember . . .*
- *I really don't like . . .*

- *What matters most to me is . . .*
- *I am really afraid of . . .*
- *I would be happy if . . .*
- *I am . . .*
- *I don't want to write today because . . .*

When you start keeping a meditation journal, your entries can be quite brief. In fact, they can always be brief—or they can be as detailed as you want to make them. Remember, your journal is not an obligation; it is a tool that can be used in a variety of ways to make your mindfulness practice work more easily. And it is always important to remind yourself that the practice of mindfulness is not about the results, but about the *practice*. The results will come, but your focus must always be on returning to the moment—your experience of the here and now, and your nonjudgmental acceptance of that experience.

Mindfulness and Everyday Issues

Bringing mindfulness into everyday life allows us to be present and perceive more accurate information about events occurring around us. We are no longer captive to the past—old habits, long-standing expectations, worn-out assumptions—and are more able to be flexible and to respond to events as they unfold. Some everyday mindfulness practices are well adapted to specific issues and concerns that we might be facing. These practices can help us bring our awareness to those issues and develop a different relationship with the thoughts, feelings, and emotions that surround them. We can notice our stress and not get stressed out; we can experience our anxiety and learn to let it go.

But it is important to remember that mindfulness is not a magic switch that you can turn on and free your brain. You must build the mindfulness muscle with intention and practice—not just when you are in a situation where you feel the need, but repeatedly and regularly. Then you won't be struggling to practice when you want to solve a problem; it will be second nature. Mindfulness practice will be the way you live your life.

In chapter 5, you learned some simple meditations to address common concerns. This chapter will revisit these topics from the perspective of practicing everyday mindfulness.

Stress

Feeling stressed out? Stop and breathe. You have learned to connect to your breath during meditation when you're distracted or distressed by thoughts or feelings, but you can also do it as you go about your daily activities. You might even want to use cues to remind you to focus on your breathing:

- Breathe when you hear the phone ring.
- Breathe when you're stopped at a red light.
- Breathe before you go into a meeting.
- Breathe when you walk to the car.
- Breathe when you put on your coat.
- Breathe while you're waiting in line.

Focusing on your breathing helps bring your awareness to your body and away from whatever thoughts are contributing to your stressful feelings. It also allows your body to be more relaxed and short-circuits the fight-or-flight feedback loop, where your body reacts to a stressful thought and then your physical reactions tell your mind that you *should* be alarmed. Your breath is always with you. You can use it anytime and anywhere.

Focusing on your body is another way to get out of the stress-response cycle. It redirects your attention to your immediate experience and allows you to concentrate on what is happening in your body.

- Focus on your feet when you walk to your car.

- Focus on your shoulders while you sit at your desk.

- Focus on your hands on the wheel while you sit at a traffic light.

- Focus on your skin as you take a shower.

You can pause in the midst of many activities to connect to your physical sensations. Try doing this while you prepare a meal, write a report, or send a text message. Shifting your awareness to your physical sensations can help you ground your experience and let go of reflexive reactivity.

Lack of Focus

Mindfulness is a powerful antidote to a lack of focus. Whether we are experiencing lack of focus as a general state of mind or we can't get ourselves to focus on a particular activity that is before us at that moment, mindfulness can offer techniques to help us harness our mental energy and concentrate.

Once again, use the breath, that most powerful tool for focusing. It can help even more if you not only pay attention to the breath, but also use an additional anchor—counting—to support your concentration. One traditional way of maintaining focus on the breath is to silently say as you breathe, "Inhale, exhale." And each time you say, "Inhale, exhale," count the number of breaths you have taken, beginning with one. So you say to yourself, "Inhale, exhale, one," and then "Inhale, exhale, two," and so on. When you notice that you are distracted from your breath, begin the count again at one.

If you reach ten, begin again at one. It's very unusual for anyone to actually get to ten without having to remind themselves again to focus on the breath. In fact, it can be difficult to get past two or three. The number of breaths you count is not important. What matters is continuing to direct your focus to the breath, using the words, the count, and the breath itself to enhance your awareness.

Doing this exercise briefly several times a day can help you develop the ability to focus. And doing it when you're having a particularly difficult time focusing can allow you to settle your mind and body before you return to the task at hand.

Anxiety

The next time you notice yourself experiencing your familiar cues of anxiety, make the choice to mindfully pause, breathe, and stay in the present moment. Then try one of the following exercises.

1. Ask yourself these questions:

   - What are my physical sensations right now?

   - What are my thoughts right now?

   - Can I let go of these physical sensations?

   - Can I accept these thoughts as just thoughts?

2. Refocus on the present, using attention to your senses of hearing, touch, and sight to allow your body and mind to shift from its agitated state to a more aware, calm condition. Take a few breaths and ask yourself one of these questions.

   - What are three things I can hear? (clock ticking, traffic going by, music in the next room, my breath)

- What are three things I can see? (this picture, that sign, that person walking by)
- What are three things I can feel? (the chair under me, the floor under my feet, my phone in my pocket)

When you have focused on the experience of one of your senses, just allow your awareness to rest there briefly, without judgment or evaluation. Focus again on your breath.

You can also use these questions even when you're not anxious. Try them at any time during the day when you just want to continue your mindfulness practice.

You can use the technique of mental noting (see page 76) when you find yourself ruminating on a problem with repetitive, nonproductive worrying instead of constructive problem solving.

Every time you notice that you are worrying in this way, make the mental note "just worrying" and refocus on your breath. Every time you catch yourself worrying, just note it again and refocus. It doesn't matter if you make a mental note ten times in one minute, or if you've been worrying for a couple hours before actually noticing and applying the technique. The important thing is that you use mental noting when you become aware that you are worrying. Using the technique involves no criticism and no effort to stop worrying; it is merely a simple, nonjudgmental noting of your state of mind.

Negative Thought Patterns

Negative thought patterns can foster destructive relationships with our acquaintances, colleagues, friends, loved ones, and even with ourselves. In theory, we can simply acknowledge the ridiculous or negative thoughts that pop into our minds, and then let them go. With negative thoughts, we can also use the technique of mental noting and when those thoughts come up, note them as "just criticizing." But negative thoughts, particularly when we are beginning a mindfulness practice, can have a hold that is difficult to release. We may be able to liberate our thoughts when we are focusing during meditation, but our efforts can be less successful during daily activities.

Rather than trying to free our minds of the negative thoughts, it is sometimes easier to replace them. One thought pattern that can supplant negativity is a mind-set of open and receptive curiosity. Consider how a young child or an animal approaches the world. They are connected to their experience in the present. Imagine that you are approaching your life in this way.

Start by picking something that might have intrigued you when you were a kid—a flower, a rock, the bark of a tree. Allow yourself to be drawn into the pattern, color, and texture. Explore all the characteristics and notice how easily you can regain a sense of wonder. Each day you can select something to approach in this way—first, objects; then as you develop your curiosity strength, you can extend the exploratory attitude to events or people, and eventually to thoughts.

When you encounter a negative thought, you don't have to hold on to it or push it away. You can approach it with the idea that it is a new experience that you want to explore with childlike wonder. You might ask, *What is this? Where did it come from? What can I learn about it?* The thought will be the subject of your investigation and remain what it is: just a thought.

Insomnia

Insomnia is often part of a negative feedback loop: not being able to get to sleep leads to worry, which leads to more insomnia, which leads to greater worry, and on and on. The regular practice of mindfulness meditation has been shown to have a positive effect on insomnia. So whenever you can during the day, take a mindfulness break.

You can do this even when you wake up in the morning. Before you get out of bed, take a few deep breaths and focus your attention on your breathing. As thoughts about the day ahead start crowding into your consciousness, focus your awareness on the pattern of your breathing and keep bringing your attention back to that focus. Just a brief mindfulness session can help start the day in a more relaxed state of mind.

As you continue through the day, look for other opportunities for a mindfulness pause. Instead of a coffee break, take a mindfulness break. Use your lunch hour for mindfulness practice, perhaps mindful eating or a mindfulness walk. As you sit at your desk or perform work tasks in the afternoon, scan your body for the physical sensations you are experiencing and allow yourself to let go of tension and tightness.

The more you practice mindfulness, the easier it will be to access when you're stressed or worried. So practicing mindfulness regularly during the day can help you be more relaxed when nighttime comes, as well as be able to implement practices that can help you let go of intrusive thoughts when it's time to sleep.

If you're having trouble sleeping, you can:

- Turn your attention to your breathing, feeling the rise and fall of your abdomen as you focus on your breath.

- Try the Body Scan Meditation (page 64) as you lie in bed. If you have been trying to get to sleep for a while, or you have awakened during the night, it is sometimes advisable to get out of bed rather than stay there, reinforcing your worry about not sleeping. So do the Body Scan Meditation while seated on a comfortable chair or couch and allow your body to relax and rest without the pressure to fall asleep.

- Use counting techniques to focus your attention. You can count your inhalations and exhalations as you bring your awareness to your breath. This is a mindfulness version of counting sheep. You can also count the different sounds you hear as you lie in bed: traffic in the street, someone moving in the household, music in another room. Make what you might see as an interference with sleep become part of your practice.

- Get up and do the Walking Meditation (page 72) to help free some of the tension in your body and mind.

Practicing Gratitude

For most people, some measure of dissatisfaction, disillusionment, and sadness is normal and temporary. Wanting something more or wanting something different can even be a catalyst for change and positive action. Yet, feelings of dissatisfaction can frequently linger on and on and pollute our entire existence.

Mindfulness practice can counteract chronic dissatisfaction via awareness and nonjudgmental acceptance. With awareness, we are able to see our thoughts not as controlling and powerful, but as just thoughts. With nonjudgmental acceptance, we assume an almost transformative perspective: we can allow both ourselves and others just to be, and find joy and peace in that acceptance.

One of the most powerful mindfulness methods for counteracting dissatisfaction is practicing gratitude. Using this simple technique, you list, either mentally or in writing, things for which you are grateful. You can do this in a variety of ways, including the following:

- **Gratitude morning.** When you're having breakfast, name three things for which you are grateful. These things can be as expansive as *I'm grateful to be alive this moment*, or as precise as *I'm grateful for how warm this tea is*. Starting the day with a gratitude exercise can set a positive tone for the rest of the day.

- **Gratitude walk.** Take a walk and see how many things you can appreciate: a blue sky, colorful fruits on a stand, a handsome dog, a majestic tree.

- **Gratitude focus.** Look around and notice something that gives you pleasure. Keep your attention on this object and experience how wonderful it is—its beauty, its utility, its delightfulness. Let the good feeling grow.

- **Gratitude journaling.** Before going to bed each night, use your journal to write a list of five things for which you're grateful. The list can include both rare and simple joys.

Once you're experiencing the many benefits of mindfulness, you may wish to expand on it. The next section of this book will help you build on the fundamentals and take your mindfulness practice to the next level.

PART THREE

A Deeper Practice

I am larger and better than I thought.
I did not know I held so much goodness.

—Walt Whitman, "Song of the Open Road"

CHAPTER SEVEN

More Advanced Meditations

As you continue to do mindfulness meditation regularly and integrate mindfulness into your daily life, you may want to deepen your practice and add to your routines. This can be accomplished by modifying the meditations you're already using and incorporating new exercises into your practice.

Deepening Your Meditations

Advanced Mindfulness Meditation (Breath Meditation)

As you become more accustomed to the practice of Follow the Breath Meditation, or Breath Meditation (page 50), you should continue to follow the following basic procedures:

- Sit in your preferred meditation posture.

- Straighten your back as if stacking one vertebra on top of another.

- Relax your shoulders, keep your head evenly balanced, and tuck your chin slightly down.

- Close your eyes or gaze downward.

- Focus your mind on the rising and falling of your breath.

- Whenever your mind wanders, gently bring it back to the awareness of your breath flowing in and out.

In order to facilitate the flow of your breath and the movement of your energy, you may also:

- Let your tongue lightly touch your palate.

- Relax your face.

- Bring attention to the small triangular area between your upper lip and nostrils, and feel every in-breath and out-breath.

If you have become experienced at following your breath, you may decide to suspend identifying and counting your inhalations and exhalations; now you just attend to the breath in its natural rhythm. You can try imagining the breath entering and exiting through a small opening an inch or two below your navel. If you begin to get sleepy, bring your focus higher, such as at the nostrils.

When you are distracted by sounds around you and thoughts within, acknowledge them and let them go, and focus again on your breath. If you want to scratch or wiggle to relieve discomfort, try letting those sensations go just as you let your thoughts go. You may find that moving your attention back to your breathing will work for physical sensations as well as thoughts. Close the meditation with your attention focused on your breathing.

Advanced Body Scan Meditations

When you're able to practice the basic Body Scan Meditation (page 64) with ease, attending to all your body parts in the customary order, you can use the following advanced procedure:

- Sit in your preferred meditation posture.

- Straighten your back as if stacking one vertebra on top of another.

- Relax your shoulders, keep your head evenly balanced, and tuck your chin slightly down.

- Close your eyes or gaze downward.

- Focus your mind on the rising and falling of your breath.

- Scan your body in large areas rather than detailed parts. For example, scan the front of your feet and legs, then the back of your feet and legs.

- Go up and down scanning large areas of your body several times until you are able to do it with fewer distractions.

- Scan the whole front of your body (head to toe) in one sweep.

- Scan the entire back of your body as one area.

- Continue with these large sweeps until you can scan this way with ease.

- Close the meditation by focusing again on your breath.

For an even more advanced version of the Body Scan Meditation, follow these steps:

- Sit in your preferred meditation posture.

- Straighten your back as if stacking one vertebra on top of another.

- Relax your shoulders, keep your head evenly balanced, and tuck your chin slightly down.

- Close your eyes or gaze downward.

- Focus your mind on the rising and falling of your breathing.

- Focus on one small area of your body as though you were pinpointing it with a laser. Bring all your attention there. Continue to focus until you feel all your awareness resting in that single spot.

- Imagine that a subtle energy like the wind is going through your body, as if there are no barriers and you have no sense of muscles or bones or organs.

- Close the meditation by focusing again on your breathing.

As you do these meditations, consider yourself to be a neutral observer and do not focus on one sensation more than another. They are simply sensations. You might itch or feel subtle sensations, pain or numbness, or perspiration. Just notice. As thoughts arise during the meditation, simply note each one as a thought and continue bringing your attention to the scanned area. Do not describe or evaluate or try to suppress your thoughts and sensations. If you have difficulty feeling sensations in certain areas, pause a few seconds and move onto another area. Do not be discouraged that your sensations are not uniform or even very noticeable. With time, all the sensations will rise and seem to float away.

Some of the sensations—such as numbness in a foot—might be more powerful during one round of scanning, but eventually will pass. If you experience a pain or strong numbness and need to change your position, you can do so by altering your position mindfully. Note every small moment as you change your position. As you continue to deepen your practice, try to simply observe the sense of numbness and let it pass.

If you find yourself overwhelmed by sensations, take a few deep, focused breaths to calm your mind and return to the scan. Do not be discouraged. Little by little, your mindfulness practice will become stronger and more powerful.

New Meditations

As you continue along your journey of mindfulness practice, your familiarity, confidence, and peacefulness with mindfulness meditation will grow. Remember to take things at your own pace, but when you feel ready, try adding any or all of these new meditations to your mindfulness practice. If you are keeping a mindfulness journal, use stream-of-consciousness writing to create a record of your experience with each new meditation. Later, simply notice if there is a shift in your experience and your relationship with your thoughts as you continue to practice new meditations.

Inner Smile Meditation

The Inner Smile Meditation connects you to your compassion and empathy. It may seem a little awkward at first, but if you are able to focus your attention, it will gradually feel more natural.

- Sit in your preferred meditation posture.

- Straighten your back as if stacking one vertebra on top of another.

- Relax your shoulders, keep your head evenly balanced, and tuck your chin slightly down.

- Place your tongue softly and comfortably on the area of your palate just above your top teeth.

- Close your eyes or gaze downward.

- Focus your mind on the rising and falling of your breath.

- Start by relaxing your face; loosen your jaw muscles, cheeks, chin, lips, eyes, and even ears. Feel all the parts of your face and head becoming calm and relaxed.

- Turn the corners of your mouth upward in a slow, gentle smile.

- Imagine you are smiling within as you start smiling with your mouth. If the feeling does not come easily, remind yourself of any experience of natural joy—for example, the face of a happy child or a smiling loved one.

- With your eyes still closed, "see" your eyes smiling.

- Next move your awareness to your cheeks, chin, and ears, and allow them to smile.

- Once you have the inner smile established in your face and head, move down to your neck and let it smile, too.

- Slowly, allow the smiling feeling to spread through your body—shoulders, arms, hands, chest, and so on—until your whole body is filled with the feeling of smiling.

- Experience every body part and internal organ smiling—brain, throat, lungs, heart, stomach, and so on. Let your attention rest briefly in each spot as you bring a smile to it.

- Bring your awareness to the warm, peaceful energy radiating within your body.

- Remain with this awareness for a period of time, bringing your attention back to your smile whenever it wanders.

- Take a few deep breaths to close the meditation.

Laughing Meditation

When we laugh, we give ourselves over to the immediacy of the present moment. We also are able to momentarily transcend minor physical and mental stresses. Although at first it may seem like a peculiar form of mindfulness meditation, laughter meditation can start the day with a joyful quality or act as a powerful relaxant at night. It can help us perceive previously unnoticed absurdities that can make life seem less solemn. There are three stages to the laughter meditation.

1. Stretching (1 to 5 minutes)
   - Stretch your whole body by standing on your toes and pulling your arms above your head with the fingers of

your two hands intertwined. Continue a catlike stretch throughout your body.

- Loosen and stretch the muscles of your jaw and face—yawn or make some funny faces.

2. Laughing (5 to 10 minutes)

- Gently turn the corners of your mouth upward and start smiling softly.

- Broaden your smile and start laughing without exerting any force. Imagine a humorous situation, remember funny jokes, or think about how odd it is to be laughing by yourself. When the giggles start to rise, let them.

- Let your laughter deepen so you feel it from your belly. If your laughter leads to physical movement, let it.

- Bring mindful awareness to the moment of laughter—whatever you experience in the moment, laugh with it. Keep on laughing until you naturally stop.

3. Stillness (5 minutes)

- Still your body. If you were standing while laughing, find a place to sit.

- Focus on your breath.

- Become aware of the silence.

- Focus briefly on any feelings or physical sensations and let them go, refocusing on your breath.

- Take a few deep breaths and close the meditation.

TIP *Because laughter can be contagious, it's sometimes easier to practice this meditation with others initially. You can also use CDs or downloaded audio files to help provide laughing stimulation.*

Loving Kindness Meditation

We often begin the practice of mindfulness meditation motivated by thoughts, feelings, or experiences we want to get rid of—anxiety, negativity, stress, pain, sleeplessness, dissatisfaction. As our practice develops, however, we can find our focus shifting, and rather than just minimizing distress, we notice the space for enhancing life.

The Loving Kindness Meditation (sometimes known as the Befriending Meditation) encourages awareness of our capacity to care for ourselves and others. We practice extending benevolent thoughts as well as acknowledging our own humanity and how that humanity connects us all. This meditation gives us a deeper appreciation of ourselves and the world around us. It's not universal approval, but rather universal acceptance. It's the ability to see vulnerability even in strangers, and suffering even in those we may find difficult. It allows us to welcome our own joy and share in the happiness of others.

Like other mindfulness practices, loving kindness can be learned. In addition to a basic Loving Kindness Meditation, there are specific loving kindness practices for situations that may require a special focus.

Basic Loving Kindness Meditation

It's best not to do this meditation if you are tired, agitated, or pressed for time. Rather, with loving kindness toward yourself, practice this meditation when you will be able to relax and experience it without additional tension or stress. The meditation—starting with yourself and systematically sending loving kindness from person to person in the described order—will have the effect of breaking down the barriers in your mind between the various categories of people and yourself, and help reduce some sources of conflict.

- Set aside at least one half hour. Find a location where there is minimal distraction.

- Sit in your preferred meditation posture.

- Straighten your back as if stacking one vertebra on top of another.

- Relax your shoulders, keep your head evenly balanced, and tuck your chin slightly down.

- Place your tongue softly and comfortably on the area of your palate just above your top teeth.

- Close your eyes or gaze downward.

- Focus your mind on the rising and falling of your breath.

- Allow yourself to settle into a comfortable pose and spend a few moments relaxing any physical tension you are experiencing. Continue to focus on your breath, allowing any distracting thoughts to float away.

- Begin by focusing on giving loving kindness to yourself. The customary phrases used in this meditation are: "May I be safe. May I be well. May I be happy. May I be peaceful and at ease."

- Thoughts and sensations will arise. In this meditation, the object of focus is not your breath, but the phrases you use to give loving kindness. Continue to return your focus to these phrases: "May I be safe. May I be well. May I be happy. May I be peaceful and at ease."

- You may find it difficult to give yourself loving kindness. The meditation may feel awkward or mechanical. You may experience thoughts that are not loving or kind. If this happens, it is especially important to be patient, allowing whatever arises to be received in a spirit of curiosity and acceptance. Continue repeating the phrases: "May I be safe. May I be well. May I be happy. May I be peaceful and at ease."

TIP *If you experience difficulty giving yourself loving kindness, it may help to picture yourself in a happy moment, or as a child or an infant, and give loving kindness to that mental image of who you are. Or try sending loving kindness to a loved one, like your pet, and then redirect the loving kindness to yourself.*

- Check your posture, notice your breath, relax any tension or tightness.

- Now call to mind someone who has helped or been kind to you—perhaps a close family member, a good friend, an inspirational figure, a teacher. Picture that person in your mind. Really see them. Now extend the loving kindness wishes to them: "May you be safe. May you be well. May you be happy. May you be peaceful and at ease."

- You may experience a variety of thoughts about this person: *They're not always so great,* or *Why would they even want my good wishes?* Just notice the thoughts and return your focus to the phrases: "May you be safe. May you be well. May you be happy. May you be peaceful and at ease."

- Check your posture, notice your breath, relax any tension or tightness.

- Now bring your attention to someone with whom you have no strong associations—perhaps a neighbor or a shopkeeper. Extend your loving kindness to that person: "May you be safe. May you be well. May you be happy. May you be peaceful and at ease."

- You may wonder why you should bother to send this person your loving kindness. But allow yourself to get a real mental picture and feel the connection to a neutral person in your life. Just notice the thoughts and return your focus to the phrases:

"May you be safe. May you be well. May you be happy. May you be peaceful and at ease."

- Check your posture, notice your breath, relax any tension or tightness.

- Now bring your attention to someone in your life whom you find difficult—perhaps a boss or a sometimes friend. Try to send loving kindness to that person: "May you be safe. May you be well. May you be happy. May you be peaceful and at ease."

TIP *When you are developing the practice of loving kindness, you may want to begin with a difficult person who does not have a strong impact on you—perhaps someone you find annoying or frustrating, rather than someone who is hostile or is bringing you pain.*

- When you begin practicing the loving kindness meditation, you may not be able to sincerely send loving kindness to this person. If you cannot, return your focus (without judgment or criticism) to sending loving kindness to yourself: "May I be safe. May I be well. May I be happy. May I be peaceful and at ease."

TIP *The following techniques may help you extend loving kindness.*

Visualizing. *Bring up a mental picture. See yourself or the person to whom the feeling is directed smiling back at you or just being relaxed.*

Reflecting. *Reflect on the positive qualities of a person or the acts of kindness they have done, even those whom you don't know well or perhaps dislike:* They seem patient with their customers, *or* He may be short with me, but he is nice to his daughter. *For yourself, make an affirmation, a positive statement about yourself, using your own words.*

Hearing. *Repeat the internalized phrase aloud:* "May I be safe. May I be well. May I be happy. May I be peaceful and at ease."

- After you have sent loving kindness to yourself and those you know, you may extend it to others with whom you are not acquainted—from all the neighbors on your street to all people and animals in all places in the universe: "May they be safe. May they be well. May they be happy. May they be peaceful and at ease."

- Take a few deep breaths and close the meditation.

The practice of loving kindness should be incorporated in everyday life in a balanced and thoughtful way. It doesn't help to be accepting of others if we exhaust or ignore ourselves in the process. But repeating the loving kindness phrases—"May I be safe," and "May you be safe," and so on—will help give us an attitude that can powerfully enhance our positive emotions.

As we go through each day, we can be mindful of how we could, even in small ways, cultivate our own safety, health, well-being, and sense of ease. And we can extend that thoughtfulness, even in small ways, to the safety, health, well-being, and ease of others. Applying the practice to daily life is a matter of directing a friendly attitude and having openness toward everyone to whom you relate, without discrimination. This is loving kindness mindfulness in action.

Some loving kindness meditations help us direct our attention in specific ways. These include the Meditation on Difficult People, Meditation on Self-Criticism, and Meditation on Positive Feelings that follow.

Meditation on Difficult People

The Meditation on Difficult People begins with the same process as the Loving Kindness Meditation on page 108.

- Set aside at least one half hour. Find a location where there is minimal distraction.

- Sit in your preferred meditation posture.

- Straighten your back as if stacking one vertebra on top of another.

- Relax your shoulders, keep your head evenly balanced, and tuck your chin slightly down.

- Place your tongue softly and comfortably on the area of your palate just above your top teeth.

- Close your eyes or gaze downward.

- Focus your mind on the rising and falling of your breath.

- Allow yourself to settle into a comfortable pose and spend a few moments relaxing any physical tension you are experiencing. Continue to focus on your breath, allowing any distracting thoughts to float away.

- Begin by focusing on giving loving kindness to yourself. Customary phrases used in this meditation are: "May I be safe. May I be well. May I be happy. May I be peaceful and at ease."

- When you feel settled and relaxed, select a person you may consider difficult and with whom you are currently experiencing problems. You may want to start with someone only mildly difficult to you, because you want to develop the practice without being overwhelmed by emotions. You need time and sufficient practice before you address major conflicts.

- Address the phrases "May you be safe. May you be well. May you be happy. May you be peaceful and at ease," to this person. Try to picture them receiving this message. You may experience anger, frustration, or a variety of negative emotions as you attempt to send loving kindness to this person. Try to reflect on how negative emotions have created limits in your own life. Breathe and repeat the phrases: "May you be safe. May you be well. May you be happy. May you be peaceful and at ease."

- Bring your focus to any positive qualities or actions of which you are aware about this person. Do they perform charitable acts? Are they nice to their animal companion? Are they always polite? Then visualize them in a positive moment and repeat the phrases: "May you be safe. May you be well. May you be happy. May you be peaceful and at ease."

- You may have to modify the phrasing you use to send loving kindness to this person in order to allow you to send it with sincerity. For example, you might say, "May you be free of envy and find peace," or "May you be filled with loving kindness." Allow yourself to send these wishes without judgment or criticism. Allow yourself to relax your heart.

- Further allow yourself to accept that this is a process that may take time and patience. Send yourself loving kindness by saying: "May I be safe. May I be well. May I be happy. May I be peaceful and at ease."

- Take a few deep breaths and close the meditation.

Meditation on Self-Criticism

- Sit in your preferred meditation posture.

- Straighten your back as if stacking one vertebra on top of another.

- Relax your shoulders, keep your head evenly balanced, and tuck your chin slightly down.

- Place your tongue softly and comfortably on the area of your palate just above your top teeth.

- Close your eyes or gaze downward.

- Focus your mind on the rising and falling of your breath.

- Allow yourself to settle into a comfortable pose, and spend a few moments relaxing any physical tension you are experiencing. Continue to focus on your breath, allowing any distracting thoughts to float away.

- Bring your awareness to a troubling emotion that you felt recently—perhaps anger, jealousy, or fear.

- Explore your thoughts and feelings about that emotion. Are you ashamed of it? Do you think you should have been able to avoid it? Do you think you are weak, bad, or foolish because you experienced it?

- Bring your attention to your body. Are you feeling any tightness or tension? If so, notice where you are experiencing the tension.

- Now change the labels you put on your feelings. Bring loving kindness to your thoughts about them. Instead of "weak," you can say "vulnerable"; instead of "bad," say "suffering"; instead of "foolish," say "hopeful."

- Bring your attention to your body and allow your breath to relax the tension. Observe any changes in your body that you may have experienced when you approached your emotions with compassion rather than criticism. Observe your thoughts and release them.

- Acknowledge that negative thoughts will always arise and that the practice is not about eliminating negativity, but noticing it and letting it go.

- Take a few deep breaths and end the meditation.

Meditation on Positive Feelings

- Sit in your preferred meditation posture.

- Straighten your back as if stacking one vertebra on top of another.

- Relax your shoulders, keep your head evenly balanced, and tuck your chin slightly down.

- Place your tongue softly and comfortably on the area of your palate just above your top teeth.

- Close your eyes or gaze downward.

- Focus your mind on the rising and falling of your breath.

- Allow yourself to settle into a comfortable pose, and spend a few moments relaxing any physical tension you are experiencing. Continue to focus on your breath, allowing any distracting thoughts to float away.

- Think of one good thing you did yesterday. It can be large or small: you worked at a soup kitchen; you let a colleague borrow your pen; you helped your sister with her budget; you flossed your teeth thoroughly; you sent a thank-you note. Now think of a few more good things you did. If you can't think of anything, allow yourself to acknowledge that sitting down to meditate is a good thing.

- For a few moments, focus on each of the good things you did and savor the feeling. If you find your inner critic reprimanding you for the good feeling—*That's not such a big deal,* or *Isn't that a little conceited?*—just notice the thought and let it go.

- Now think of someone—like a friend, colleague, benefactor, or loved one—who has done a good thing for you. Think of this person's kindness and feel your appreciation.

- Think of someone you know who is having some difficulty. Think of the strengths this person has to help address their problems. Think of the resources this person has to draw on for help.

- Think of a difficult moment in your day—a distressing phone call, something that interfered with your schedule—and focus on how you handled it. Perhaps you took a few deep breaths and calmed yourself; perhaps you adjusted your commitments to fit your time realities. Allow yourself to acknowledge your strengths and recognize that most things will change. You, too, can grow and change.

- Think of someone with whom you find it challenging to interact with. See if you can think of something good this person has done. If not, just acknowledge that he or she wants to find happiness.

- Focus your attention on the phrase: "Everyone wants happiness—may we all be happy." Repeat the phrase as often as you want.

- When you are ready, take a few deep breaths and end the meditation.

Dr. Dan Siegel, co-director of the Mindful Awareness Research Center at the University of California, Los Angeles, devised the acronym *COAL*—curiosity, openness, acceptance, and love toward our ongoing experience—to describe the qualities of mindfulness. Allow yourself to remember this acronym. Perhaps even try using *COAL* as a personal mantra. Reminding ourselves of these cornerstones of practice can help us bring mindfulness to everything we do.

Mindfulness means being awake.

—Jon Kabat-Zinn, *Wherever You Go, There You Are*

CHAPTER EIGHT
A New Peace

You may agree by now that mindfulness is for everyone. Although its origins are in Eastern thought systems, it requires no religious beliefs, no philosophical tenets. It can be observed by individuals of any gender, age, or background. As you know by now, all you need to practice mindfulness are your body, your mind, and your breath.

Mindfulness involves a clear awareness of your inner world and your external environment, including thoughts, emotions, sensations, and actions as well as surroundings, as they exist in any particular moment. It requires a nonjudgmental acceptance of experience that involves noticing rather than evaluating. It develops your ability to have a large perspective or clear awareness, as well as focused attention and consciousness of details.

As you continue your mindfulness journey, going at your own pace, you will likely find that you are able to see things more clearly, respond more effectively, and experience greater balance and flexibility in your life. You know now that the practice of mindfulness has been associated with better stress management, decreased anxiety and depression, a greater sense of well-being, a reduction in sleeplessness, and an increased capacity to deal with pain. You may have already started practicing mindfulness meditation and keeping a mindfulness journal.

In the beginning of this book, you were encouraged to begin your mindfulness journey with a single step: committing to learning about the practice of mindfulness. So now it may be time to take an even bigger step: fully committing to your practice of mindfulness. Mindfulness works for you if you work at it. It's a habit that, like most things, gets easier and more accessible the more you do it. In a short time, you'll discover that mindfulness is one of the best ways to live a more peaceful and fulfilling life. Welcome to the life that you are creating for yourself through the practice of mindfulness.

RESOURCES

In addition to the tips and techniques outlined in this book, here is a list of resources for further expanding and enhancing your practice. You can even use some of them to locate a mindfulness teacher or practice group in your area.

Organizations and Teaching Centers

Center for the Advancement of Well-Being, Fairfax, Va.
http://wellbeing.gmu.edu

The Center for Contemplative Mind in Society, Northampton, Mass.
www.contemplativemind.org

Center for Investigating Healthy Minds, Madison, Wis.
www.investigatinghealthyminds.org

Center for Mindfulness at UC San Diego, San Diego, Calif.
http://health.ucsd.edu/specialties/mindfulness/pages/default.aspx

The Center for Mindfulness, Fresno, Calif.
www.thecenterformindfulness.com

Center for Mindfulness in Medicine, Health Care,
and Society, Worcester, Mass.
www.umassmed.edu/cfm/index.aspx

Common Ground Meditation Center, Minneapolis, Minn.
www.commongroundmeditation.org

Duke Integrative Medicine, Durham, N.C.
www.dukeintegrativemedicine.org

Garrison Institute, Garrison, N.Y.
www.garrisoninstitute.org

Insight Meditation Society, Barre, Mass.
www.dharma.org

Mind & Life Institute, Hadley, Mass.
www.mindandlife.org

Mindful Living Programs, Chico, Calif.
www.mindfullivingprograms.com

Mindfulness Awareness Research Center (MARC) at UCLA,
Los Angeles, Calif.
http://marc.ucla.edu

The Mindfulness-Based Campus-Community Health Program,
Little Rock, Ark.
www.ualr.edu/mindfulness

Mindfulness Meditation New York Collaborative, New York, N.Y.
www.mindfulnessmeditationnyc.com

OpenMind Training Institute, Santa Monica, Calif.
www.ronaldalexander.com

Penn Program for Mindfulness, Philadelphia, Pa.
www.pennmedicine.org/stress

Santa Fe Vipassana Sangha, Santa Fe, N.M.
www.santafevipassana.org

University of Minnesota Center for Spirituality & Healing,
Minneapolis, Minn.
www.csh.umn.edu

Books, Publications, and CDs

Rick Hanson, *Buddha's Brain: The Practical Neuroscience of Happiness, Love, and Wisdom*

Sharon L. Horstead, *Living the Mindful Way: 85 Everyday Mindfulness Practices for Finding Inner Peace*

Jon Kabat-Zinn, *Full Catastrophe Living: Using the Wisdom of Your Body and Mind to Face Stress, Pain, and Illness*

Jon Kabat-Zinn, *Mindfulness for Beginners: Reclaiming the Present Moment—and Your Life*

Sharon Salzberg, *Real Happiness: The Power of Meditation: A 28-Day Program*

Daniel J. Siegel, *The Mindful Brain: Reflection and Attunement in the Cultivation of Well-Being*

Ronald D. Siegel, *The Mindfulness Solution: Everyday Practices for Everyday Problems*

Thích Nhất Hạnh, *Peace Is Every Step: The Path of Mindfulness in Everyday Life*

Thích Nhất Hạnh, *The Miracle of Mindfulness: An Introduction to the Practice of Meditation*

Websites

The Center for Contemplative Mind in Society guided meditation downloads
www.contemplativemind.org/practices/recordings

Deer Park Monastery: "The Five Mindfulness Trainings"
http://deerparkmonastery.org/mindfulness-practice/
the-five-mindfulness-trainings

Discussions on the basics of mindfulness practice
www.audiodharma.org/talks/?search=mindful

Google Tech Talks video on "The Cognitive Neuroscience of
Mindfulness Meditation"
www.youtube.com/watch?v=sf6QoG1iHBI

Guided meditations and selected talks
www.dharma.org/resources/audio

Mindful
www.mindful.org

Mindfulnet
www.mindfulnet.org

Plumline: "The 14 Mindfulness Trainings"
http://plumline.org/practice/the-14-mindfulness-trainings

Shambhala Sun
www.shambhalasun.com

Sounds True's interactive guides to meditation
www.soundstrue.com/guide/

"STOP: A Short Mindfulness Practice" by Elisha Goldstein and Bob Stahl
www.youtube.com/watch?v=PhwQvEGmF_I

Talk and guided meditation by Jon Kabat-Zinn at Google
www.youtube.com/watch?v=3nwwKbM_vJc

"Thich Nhat Hanh's Five Mindfulness Trainings"
http://buddhism.about.com/od/Morality/a/Thich-Nhat-Hanh-S-Five-
Mindfulness-Trainings.htm

University of Missouri–Columbia Mindfulness Practice Center's guided
mindfulness practice audio/video
www.umsystem.edu/curators/wellness/wellness_video

Vipassanā Fellowship: "Mindfulness in Plain English"
www.vipassana.com/meditation/mindfulness_in_plain_english_7.php

INDEX

JOURNAL

_____

_____

_____

_____

_____

_____

_____

_____

_____

_____

_____

_____

_____

_____

_____

_____

_____

_____

_____

CPSIA information can be obtained
at www.ICGtesting.com
Printed in the USA
BVHW040617290323
661296BV00012B/66